WOMEN THRIVE

VOLUME II

INSPIRING TRUE STORIES OF WOMEN OVERCOMING ADVERSITY

RAIMONDA JANKUNAITE   POLI SEVCIKOVA
CHRISTELLE PILLOT   LAUREN J. BUCKNER
CARMEN BENTON   PAIGE FRISONE
KATRINA MARSH   BETH A. BOLES

WOMEN THRIVE MEDIA LTD

COPYRIGHT

This book compilation is initiated by Raimonda Jankunaite, the founder of Women Thrive Media Ltd. If you would like to be published as an author in our future book compilations such as this please visit www.womenthrivesummit.com/book or email us at contact@womenthrivemedia.com

Paperback ISBN: 978-1-7384107-0-5

Ebook ISBN: 978-1-7384107-1-2

Cover Art: Rajni Chunara @Lineart_ly

Cover Design: Samantha Pearce from SWATT

With thanks to Trudy Simmons, Tracie Couper, Tonya Whittington, Rachel West and Abigail Pugh and the whole Women Thrive Media team for their support in bringing this book to life.

DEDICATION

This book is dedicated to you, the woman who aspires for more in life. A woman who knows that despite your pains and struggles, you are meant for more. A woman who wants to thrive and is inspired by other women rising to their power and purpose in life.

For a woman who wants to become aligned, live a purposeful life and create the freedom to be who she was created to be. Be unapologetically you.

"A butterfly cannot see its wings, but the rest of us can. Remember: you are beautiful, and while you may not see it, we can."

Do you feel inspired to share highlights of this book on social media? We would love for you to use hashtag #WomenThriveBook and tags us @womenthrivemedia

To get to know our authors and to get access to special gifts from each author, please visit www.womenthrivesummit.com/book

CONTENTS

WHY THIS BOOK EXISTS

At Women Thrive Media, our mission is to create a stage where every woman can have the opportunity to shine. A place where she can share her story and, by doing so, inspire others. Every single one of those stories deserves to be told and heard.

Over the years, we have had the privilege to meet thousands of incredible women through in-person and virtual events and every woman had a story to share. In our work, we have had the opportunity to spotlight close to a thousand women across our event stages and podcast and we are yet to share more incredible stories in the years to come.

This book is the second volume of our WOMEN THRIVE anthologies. We believe that writing your story in a book is so much more magical and personal than simply speaking; the words we write on paper live on forever, possessing an immortal power. We hope this book finds space on your bookshelf, bedside chest of drawers, coffee table, or library alongside other inspirational books.

The process of writing your story is a beautiful one, healing and liberating. It is healing and liberating for the readers *and* the authors themselves. We learned that the very act of writing your story can in itself be transformative and create so many opportunities for personal and spiritual growth. In the words of our authors, this has been one of the most healing and transformational journeys, in simply recalling and reflecting on their life's experiences. Today, you as a reader get to be the witness of their final works.

Through our WOMEN THRIVE book series, we hope to give as many women the opportunity to write their stories in a book and inspire the world with words of encouragement. Sharing stories of overcoming adversities in life, and finding the way forward to rise and thrive.

If you would like to contribute to our future Women Thrive Book series, please visit www.womenthrivesummit.com/book, where you will find our interest form.

On our website, you will find video interviews with every speaker from the Women Thrive Podcast. You can also find us on most podcast streaming platforms by searching Women Thrive. This is a fantastic opportunity to get to know our speakers and hear more about their journeys as authors in this book.

INTRODUCTION

Dear Reader,

I encourage you to savour every single word in every chapter of this book, because each one has been written with the same purpose in mind – to help you thrive.

This anthology has been created by eight, amazing women from different parts of the world, backgrounds and life experiences. While they didn't know each other before investing their passion and truth into this project, they all shared something in common. And that something was a mission to positively impact others through the power of their stories.

Some of these stories have not been shared before. We thank these women for being brave enough to pour their hearts out to you, dear reader, in the hope that by doing so they'll make a positive difference in your life. It takes a lot of courage, soul searching, self-questioning and doubting to speak our truth. To lay our challenges and our trials bare for someone else to read and experience is an act of bravery that cannot be underestimated. It requires reliving our stories and committing ourselves to inner healing.

You may not resonate with all eight of these stories today,

but the story that touches you least today may be exactly the one you need to hear at some point down the road. It may hold the wisdom that you require for a future challenging experience. The purpose of this book is to inspire you and to remind you that life comes with adversities, unexpected twists and turns, and sometimes the path is very rocky indeed. There will be times when you're riding high on life, and seem to have it all. Then, life just pulls the rug out from under your feet.

This book aims to give you the strength and inspiration to KEEP GOING despite the challenges. And to triumph over adversity. For some, the start in life was not as fortunate as it could be. And, some of these women could have been stuck on a trajectory of tragedy. For others, adversity came later in life, bringing valuable lessons and teaching that purpose can be found in pain.

These authors have experienced some truly trying times that nearly broke them. But in those moments of defeat and despair, they found strength, awakening and a will of steel to survive and come through the other side. Stronger than ever. As you read the pages of this book, remember that this could be someone's survival guide. Share this guide. Gift it to your friends and loved ones. Leave a review, tell us how this book has touched your life. Send a message to an author (or authors) that have really moved you with their story.

I promise you that is the most rewarding part of writing a book. Having our readers tell us just how much our words have meant to them. It is the biggest gift and blessing to have our stories out in the world, touching people's lives.

Now, take a few moments to really look at the pictures on the cover. There may be one face that 'speaks' to you today. And the next time you hold this book in your hand, another face may resonate with you. This anthology is designed to take you on an inspirational journey, an experience where every time you read it you'll discover something new about the author, their story, or yourself.

As you tread your own path, take your own journey, may this book be a companion. And a reminder of just how strong, resilient, and capable we all are of overcoming adversities and finding our way through them, to shine and thrive.

Raimonda Jankunaite

1

THE LIFE EXPERIENCES THAT SHAPED THE WOMAN I AM TODAY

BY RAIMONDA JANKUNAITE

I was raised in a small town in Lithuania where life was quite simple when I think about it now. We didn't have worries and I lived most of my childhood outdoors with the freedom to roam around all I wanted. From an early age, I knew what freedom looked like and how magical it felt to be unrestricted. Today, freedom is still one of my core values.

Somehow, I don't think my parents ever had the need to control me and I was always pretty independent. I remember my mum saying to me every time I was being lazy about doing my homework: "Well if you don't want to do your homework you can go and milk the cows when you grow up." I knew what she meant because, in my early childhood, we were surrounded by cattle. We lived in my mother's grandparents' legacy home in a small village, and I was looked after by my mother's aunt Adele.

Adele was one of the most hard-working women I knew. She was a fantastic chef who catered for weddings and events, she would sew dresses for women, look after me, take care of the cattle and work the land. We had land as far as your eyes could see and I would roam around the grass, watch beautiful clouds, smell the flowers and feel nature under my feet all day long. This was how I knew my childhood to be.

I did not see much of my parents, who were young and worked hard, as mostly they were on the road doing various business. They were always industrious and made money doing things no one else was doing. My dad would make beer in our garage and deliver it to local weddings and parties. I remember the back of our house was filled with massive bags of shoes: red, black, brown, white, and grey. These were mid-heel sandals. Back then there was not much you could buy in the shop, so these shoes were pretty valuable and in high demand. I used to put my little feet into these pretty shoes and walk around the house imagining I was a grown-up. This was just one of my family's businesses, selling shoes to markets in Latvia.

Adele was my idol. She was a tiny, barely 5ft tall lady, with a hunchback, the sweetest smile and the kindest heart. She would help everyone she could and look after everyone's children, without having her own. She refused to marry any of the men who pursued her because her condition developed at the age of 15 and her hunchback grew to be quite big. She chose to never marry as an act of selflessness; Adele didn't want to let a husband down by not having children, and she didn't want to have children, for fear of passing on her condition.

By the time I knew Adele, she was in her 60s, hard of hearing and struggling with her eyesight, but she was smart, witty and could smell you from a mile away. She was very fair and had a lot of wisdom and so many people would come to her to seek her advice and counsel. She had long, natural hair to her ankles that she would brush every Sunday before making long plaits and tying it into a bun that she wore underneath a scarf. She would make the most delicious bakes, biscuits, pastry and other treats for us.I loved her, and I know she loved me back because when she got old and could no longer brush her hair she asked me to be the one to cut it. I knew it was a grand gesture, as she refused to go to the hair dresser and entrust me with her beloved hair. When she passed, she left me all of our ancestral land, which she knew I cherished as my home of birth which carried all of our family history.

Growing up before my time

I always wanted to grow up quickly and be with the older cool kids. But in fact, I didn't have to, life took care of that all on its own. When I was just 11 years old, things took a different turn in my life. By then we lived in the most beautiful newly-built home in the city and life was good. I went to school, and in the summer holidays, my parents would take me and my sister on vacations to the seaside and camping. I would spend summers at my grandma's house or at the village visiting Adele and do what every kid would be doing back then - having a whole lot of fun outdoors.

But this summer was different. My mum and sister had gone to London. My mum had just lost her job at the court-house and my sister had finished her mid-school. It wasn't a vacation trip, it was a trip to find a job. My sister was 15 at the time and I was close to her. Even though we used to fight some-times, she was my older sis and I was sad to see her go.

After my mum and sister left, I was taken to summer camp where I'd spend a few weeks. I didn't really know what was going on, but I was happy to spend the summer with my friends and do something I had never done before. When I got home from summer camp, my home felt empty. Mum was not there and my dad did not spend much time looking after me. He dropped me to the village where I was raised and left me with my mum's auntie Adele. I knew something was going on, my intuition told me there would be a turn of fate, but I carried on in my blissful childhood ways.

A few days later, I got the news. My dad has been locked up. I knew he had been in court, accused of running a business that was not 'above board', but we were all so sure he'd be found innocent. Instead, he'd been convicted and sentenced to two years in prison. When I got the news the reality did not sink in. I packed my bags and was driven back to my house and left on my own to get myself sorted.

As I walked in through the front door, I saw the house was a complete mess; broken glass and lots of blood on the floor, along with a strong smell of alcohol. I was so confused and didn't know what had happened. All I knew was my mum wasn't there and my dad was gone. I later found out that he'd thrown a big party after his court appearance to celebrate his victory, without knowing the verdict. Dad was so sure that he'd won the case, only to return to court the next day and discover he'd been found guilty. He was taken into custody, right there and then. The blood was from some kind of injury he sustained to his arm, while drunk, and he'd been rushed to the hospital that night to stitch his hand.

Panic overwhelmed me and, as I was packing my bags to leave and go to stay at my grandma's, tears started to run down my face. I could not bear the pain of being in a house that felt completely empty. I was having flashes of different scenarios of what had happened in our home the night before and nothing made sense. This was the moment that would later severely impact my life. The feeling of fear, emptiness and lack of safety. Being 'abandoned' created fear in my subconscious that would later manifest itself as a limiting belief that would stop me from growing my business. But it took deep subconscious work to uncover this many years later.

I walked outside and sat on the stairs at the front of the house. The big, beautiful, red brick, three-storey house, with a white staircase and perfectly manicured front garden. My parents built the house of their dreams, the most beautiful home in the area, and it was only a few years since we'd moved in. People would often walk by and slow down to look at this house that from the outside looked like we were living the dream. Now, I was alone in this house that we called home with no one to call for help. I cried for a while longer trying to gather myself so I could figure out what to do next.

Seeing the blood and glass on the floor gave me immense anxiety and being alone made me feel deep fear and hopelessness. I am quite stubborn and never ask for help, but in that moment it all got too much and I couldn't handle it on my own. My legs felt weak, but the only thing I could do was walk down to my neighbour's house and ask for help. I was alone and so scared. The neighbours followed me to my house, helped me pack and took me to my grandma's home. When I got there, reality kicked in. At the age of 11, this was my new life. So I had to grow up quickly and start figuring out things on my own.

Turns out, I was pretty good at figuring things out and playing grown-up. I was going to school, taking care of the big, old house on the weekends, running family errands, cleaning and arranging prison visits to see my dad every other month. My grandparents were looking after me but would not be too involved in the running of the errands that I knew I had to do. Occasionally, my parent's friends would come and check on me, intently looking into my eyes to see how I was coping.

One of my parent's friends, Algis, would pick me up regularly and would even take me fishing on the lake, something he knew I loved doing with my dad. He wasn't particularly good at it, but it put a smile on my face doing things that I was used to doing with my dad. Nothing replaced not having my parents around, but I didn't let myself dwell on things. I was in survival mode. I simply had to grow up and do what it took to keep on going. When you are placed in a situation that you cannot control, you accept the new reality and find a way through it. I was of course very sad, but I felt strong - like I had to rise to the occasion so my parents could be proud. I had a sense of pride in taking on life as a grown-up.

Luckily, my dad didn't have to serve his full two-year sentence and was home after 18 months. Released early for good behaviour. My mum came to welcome him home and it was surreal having my parents back. But things weren't the same. We never went back to the 'normal life' I knew before this incident. I felt like there was no going back to the innocent, careless childhood that I had prior to all of this unfolding. I felt like this was the point when my childhood was stolen away and the harsh reality of life dropped on me like a bombshell. It did not take us long to figure out that if we wanted to build a better life, we would need to migrate. Yes, we had a big beautiful home but no income to sustain it, through it all we lost all of our businesses and had to start over again. So my parents made the decision we would leave and immigrate to London where my sister was still living.

The young immigrant girl at the pizza shop

There I was, aged 13 and wheeling a suitcase bigger than myself down the Heathrow hallways, terrified that Customs wouldn't let me through to see my family. I was flying alone because my mum and dad were already in the UK. Back then, entering the UK was not so easy and being Lithuanian meant we were 'unwanted' immigrants. And so my immigrant journey began, I spoke no English and had no friends, but I had this go-getter mentality because of this early survival mode. As soon as I landed, I knew I would have to help my parents, not because they asked me to but because I knew they were working several jobs and earning minimum wage. Life was very different to what I had known before, where my parents did not always have real jobs in Lithuania, but ran their own businesses and made very good money.

The first day I was in the UK, we went for a walk. I walked into a pizza shop and asked if they needed someone to hand out flyers for their business. My English was very minimal but I could somehow communicate. I was shy but I was determined - something inside me was striving to succeed or perhaps it was to just survive. I think being an immigrant and having to do whatever jobs we could get instilled a sense of determination of 'I will do whatever it takes to succeed'. To my surprise, they said yes and told me to come back the next day. Bright and early, I was at the front door of the pizza place ready for my stack of flyers. I remember that day as if it was yesterday. I had to distribute 1,000 flyers for £20, a job that took me 4-5 hours. I carried the heavy stack in my backpack and delivered a flyer to every house in the neighbourhood. At the end of the day, my legs would be in so much pain, but it did not stop me from coming back the next day. £20 may not sound like a lot of money but that was the first money I earned myself and I was proud to spend it on anything I wanted.

My 'career' in the pizza shops had begun and when I lost one job I'd just go and find another one, and another one. I remember once I got home, and told my mum: "I got fired from my job, oh but don't worry I got another one on my way home." I would get fired mainly because when these pizza shops treated me unfairly I would chuck away their flyers and they would know I hadn't done the job. I was restless and smart but I hated injustice. At one of the shops I got promoted to answer the phones and take orders and so I worked at pizza shops until the age of 16, eventually being able to run the whole shop full of staff all on my own. The managers would leave me to run a shift and be in charge of the shop at the age of 15. I was hard working and had this sense of being in control so my managers trusted me with more responsibility than others. Despite being 'promoted' I never did actually get paid more for the role and still earned a minimum wage.

The truth is that all along I was underage to work, and at the start of my 'career' an illegal immigrant too, but no one knew and I did not always have to disclose my real age. Because I looked older and was very mature for my age I never got quizzed about it. Until one day, a co-worker started to ask me questions. Because I trusted him, I told him my real age and he asked me - why aren't you at school? I said I didn't go to school. My parents could not find me a place at school which is why I was working. The truth was that my parents were too scared to take me to school as we did not have an immigration status and could be deported at any time.

I saw the look on his face, then he asked: "How is it possible you are 14 and you don't go to school?" To me that was my new reality - go to work, earn money and take each day at a time. As long as we weren't getting deported, staying under the radar was the only way of survival. To him, this was a shock but for me, it was my life as I knew it. So he volunteered to speak to his school where he was already a senior attending the 6th form, to see if he could get me a place there.

To be honest, at the age of 14, I had already made peace that from here on it would only be work for me. I did not think I would ever finish school. But to my surprise, my co-worker came back to me a few days later and said that he'd got me a meeting with the Principal and if all was OK I would get a place there. Sure enough, I got the place. A few weeks later, I was starting school - at the beginning of the summer of year 10, with year 11 being the final year of school. I came in not expecting much but what I got from it was way more than I could have ever asked.

It was at that school that I truly learned some skills that would serve me for life. Most important to me was being surrounded by friends from diverse backgrounds, kids from all nationalities and origins. I got to be exposed to so much in such a short space of time, and I will always cherish that experience. This experience profoundly shaped my own views on diversity and multicultural backgrounds, which I'd later come to appreciate and champion in my own communities. Even though the area in which I went to school could be classed as a rough area for me, this was my school and it was the best thing that happened to me. Even more surprising to me was that I managed to pass almost all of my exams, with very minimal English. I initially failed my English language exam but I would re-take it two more times in order to pass. I was never one to give up easily, perseverance was built in me from an early age.

Passing my English exams meant I could one day go to university, and, at this stage, this was not something I could ignore. I have come this far, I could surely finish and go to university. A new hunger for education had taken hold of me and nothing was stopping me now. Not only did I pass my English exam (3rd time lucky) I also went on to study law and politics at college, business management at university, and law at post-graduate school. If I failed at something, I would try again and again until I got it. I think some of this was instilled in me through my environment and subconscious programming from my childhood.

Survival from the roots

When I was a child, I would sit with my grandma and she would tell me stories for hours of how her family survived being involuntarily taken to the depths of Siberia, Russia, during the mass deportation due to Soviet Union expansion in the 1940s. They were deported because they had more than others, such as land and cattle and therefore arrested at their home and taken away against their will. At the time Adele was out doing sowing work so she never got arrested. Their land

and home were taken by the Russian regime which they would later have to 'buy back' in order to live there again.

My grandma's family spent days if not weeks travelling in train wagons suitable only for animals, filled with other families who faced the same fate. Once in Russia, they had to start life over from nothing, living in massive barracks with other families experiencing the same adversity. They ate whatever they could find or made do when there was nothing. Grandma told me stories of making soup out of food scraps they were given and eating things that were unimaginable today. Treated like slaves and given no money for their work in the woods, where they had to chop massive trees and transport them across the river. All this while living in the harshest of climates with freezing winters reaching -30 degrees and scorching summers reaching temperatures of +40.

I spent hours asking my grandmother to share more stories like these, as it made me feel humble and in awe of just how strong my grandparents were and how much a person can endure. The ingenuity of their survival was truly admirable and humbling. My grandmother was just 16 when she and her parents and siblings were taken to Siberia, travelling for weeks to face their sentence - slaving away for more than 15 years under the Russian regime. Grandma also left school just before her exams and never finished her education. When she got arrested she asked the officer if she should pack her books, as she wanted to sit her final exams, only to be told that she will not need them again. It is ironic that at roughly the same age, I was in a similar situation living as an immigrant and starting to work with no hope of ever finishing school. My life was nothing short of ordinary but we had this survival instinct that would get us through just about anything. From all those stories my grandma told me, surviving the war and the harshest conditions working in the woods, I knew there was nothing I could not conquer, I was already built for survival.

£5 in your pocket

I remember when my sister was pregnant at the age of 23 and I was 17. By this time, I was no longer working at the pizza shops and had upgraded to working at estate agents. One day after work I remember meeting my mum and sister in our little Seat Ibiza car and driving to view properties, with the aim of buying one. Well, that day my mum had £5 to put fuel in the car, which is equivalent to approx a gallon or 4 litres of fuel. It was as much money as we had.

At the time, my sister was pregnant and she had already decided that she wasn't going to be with the father. We lived in Peckham, one of the rough areas in London at the time, in a shared townhouse with other tenants. One shared bathroom and a small kitchen and an extra 4 or 5 people, as well as our family of four. It was far from an ideal set-up to bring a child into the world and much different to what we knew from our big beautiful home back in Lithuania.

So, my mum decided that we were buying a house. Yes, just like that. Immigrant family, working for minimum wage, with no savings and no real prospect of getting finance, we were buying a house. That day, I remember very vividly us walking into this particular house and my mum saying: "We are buying this house." It was £250,000, not a small amount for a family who had £5 to their name at the time. But my mum was no quitter and she would always make the impossible work. Her sheer determination taught me that the impossible can be done, but it was that inner fuel of purpose that drove her to overcome any challenge in front of her.

When she got home that day, she proclaimed to my dad - "We are buying a house"! He looked at her and said - "Woman, I think you are crazy." He never supported this vision but I think it fuelled my mum's mission even further. She knew that if she did not take action, nothing would change and you can't stop my mum once she has made a decision to move. Plus, her motherly instinct was at an all-time high. She had her first granddaughter on the way and she wasn't going to let her come into this world in the conditions in which we were living. And so, 6 months later, in October a day after my mum's birthday, we were moving into our new house. We had no furniture but we were happy because we had reached our goal. Just two months before my niece would be born, in early December.

At this point, my mum and dad had gone their separate ways. On the day we were moving into our new house, my dad was moving into rented accommodation. He could not bear the fact that now my mum was the owner of the house and he was the tenant. Because he never wanted to partake in the purchase, my mum did everything she had to do to get it all on her own. It was his stubbornness and ego he could not conquer, couldn't handle no longer being the man of the house, the final voice of power. Mum had prevailed.

You see, my dad was a typical old-school man. A man who would hide his own insecurities with ego and power games, at times violence and controlling ways to keep my mum down. But my mum was a smart and strong woman, so although she didn't divorce my dad until this point, she faced a lot of struggles and heartache. It was not uncommon to see my dad 'lose it' and launch his fists at my mum. It had become my survival mechanism to not only stand up to my dad but also keep him calm and at bay when he got angry. I would stand in front of my mum facing my dad with my hands up in the air and usher him away screaming at him. His anger was mainly fuelled by the fact that my mum was more outgoing and got more attention than he did. He hated the feeling of being insignificant. My mum always had the respect of others and in any situation people would come to her for her counsel, knowing my dad was not a very friendly man and would usually shut the door in front of you.

Many years later, I asked my mum why she never walked

away when she was facing violence at home, and she told me that it was us who kept her there. What would she do with two small children, how would she take care of us, what would people think? It was the norm back in the day.

When I was young, I swore to myself that I would never repeat my mum's story or allow a man to treat me like this. She suffered a lot of physical abuse and disempowerment, which she would hide and show no weakness to anyone. Throughout my life I continued to stand up for my mum and now other women who may have been through similar experiences. I was never afraid of my dad, only afraid of what he may do to her. Living in daily fear of another fight breaking out in my house that may or not may end in fatality. What I do today in providing a safe space for women to rise is so personal; it is so entwined with my childhood experiences of observing disempowerment, helplessness and regular threats. Admittedly, my dad has changed a lot in his older age and he is a different man than he was when he was young. He is much more thoughtful, kind and loving in his old age. But, for me, it caused heaps of trauma at the time, trauma that manifested itself much later in my life.

So here we were, all girls in the house, just over a month before my niece's arrival and moving into our own new home in England. Such a surreal achievement for us as an immigrant family. At the start, we used to sleep on mattresses on the floor and eat at a plastic garden table in our dining room, before we could afford furniture. I remember my mum would take our clothes and go wash them at her clients' homes, as she worked as a cleaner. We didn't have a washing machine for a while because we couldn't afford to buy one. It was a tough few years but we made it through and, today, it is still our family house that my niece and all of us can call home.

I am so proud of my mum and also my sister who are both such strong and resilient women. Both had unwavering determination when it came to providing for our family and fighting for our safety and survival. Both my sister and my mum were the original immigrants in the UK before me and my dad arrived and they worked extra hard to get themselves set up. I will always respect my sister, who arrived in London at the age of fifteen and worked her way up to now having a degree and several successful businesses. She has always been financially strong and determined to be the breadwinner and never asked for help.

Today, 17 years later since my niece's birth, I am also now a mama to a beautiful little girl who came into this world. Now I can understand the feeling my mum had, as I have the same sense of protection and natural instinct of nurture.

Today, my mum and I live in Spain, and just a few weeks ago, we saw an apartment that I fell in love with at first sight. At first I hesitated to make an offer to buy this apartment, but remembering my mum's story I told myself that even though I may not be ready for this leap, I will make a bet on myself and make an offer on this property. I don't know exactly how I am going to find the money for it yet, but I know if my mum could do it, working as a cleaner, I know I can do it too. I am determined to pay for this property in full without the need to take out a mortgage. I have 3 months to do it, so let's see if this goal comes to fruition. I believe that through sheer determination and ingenuity, anything is possible. When you set your mind to attain a specific goal, make a plan and take inspired action, you can have it all. This is my goal, to be financially empowered and show my daughter that she can do anything she sets her mind to also. So, one day, I can tell her this story of her mama being determined to buy us a home with no financing and achieving this goal.

How do you do it all?

When people ask me today - how do you do it? How do you run your business, have a baby and find the time to do everything? I just look at them and smile. Because you have no idea that I have come from a lineage of courageous and determined women who all stood strong. They were all so resilient and, above all, kindhearted, yet facing life's challenges with purposeful stride.

Admittedly, my mum is here by my side supporting my vision and helping with looking after my daughter when I work. It really takes a team or a village to raise a baby, it's not one person's job. I can't imagine having to do it all on my own - and the truth is we don't have to. We don't have to prove to anyone that we are a superwoman by carrying the burden of everything. I know my parents relied on their parents to support them and my mum is here with me every step of the way.

Today, I also have a fantastic team of people in my business, because I knew that after giving birth I would not want to work 12 hours a day and my priorities would shift. I knew that I would also be determined more than ever to provide and create safety for my daughter and that I couldn't do it on my own. So I intentionally spent the 9 months preparing for my daughter's arrival by hiring and training people in my business. Creating processes and structures that would uphold our vision and would function without me being there.

This is easy compared to the challenges and struggles we have faced as immigrants, or the unimaginable struggles that my grandparents had to face. What I do today is easy because I am fuelled by purpose and mission.

Today, I get to support women in their businesses and help them build success for freedom. I also get to do women's empowerment work, which underpins the very core of our business today. I don't just speak about women's empowerment,

I make it part of everything we do. It is embedded in the ethos and values of what I do and how we do it as an organisation.

My vision is global, to touch the lives of women who may not have the courage or the opportunity to share their voice. I strive to build a platform for all of our stories to be heard, tread and transmuted through space and time. To touch the lives of other women, empower them and give them the strength and courage to pursue their dreams. Because I know that we all have limitless potential and opportunities.

Today we host the annual Women Thrive summit, publish a beautiful women's empowerment magazine, run a podcast and publish this very book - with the common goal to build a platform where every woman's story can be heard. My mission through it all is that women have a platform and the opportunity to share their voice and their stories with the world where their voices can be amplified. It is my mission to create a safe space for women to speak their truth.

For so long and still today, there are so many women who are disempowered, who do not have a voice, who do not have power over their finances, who have no control and fear for their safety. Women who cannot speak their truth or walk away from their circumstances. I want my work to be a testament to what women are capable of, and inspire others to become self-empowered. Because there is no one else who will give you that - only you are able to empower yourself to be strong and determined and take the lead in your own life.

In volume 1 of this book, I share my own story of self-empowerment and walking away from a similar situation that my mum faced. Breaking free from disempowerment and control and seeking my own freedom. Until today, freedom continues to be one of my core values, because I know the cost of it and how hard those before have had to fight for it.

There is nothing more important today than women being empowered and free to rise to their true essence, unlocking their potential and their true value in this world. I believe when women are empowered, we empower others, we pay it forward, we build sustainable businesses and support communities around us. That is why it is important to me that we support and empower each other, so we can do more good in this world and leave a legacy that positively impacts the next generation.

RAIMONDA JANKUNAITE

Raimonda Jankunaite is the founder of Women Thrive Media, a best-selling author, international speaker, speaking coach and visibility expert. She helps other business founders become recognised and highly visible experts and sought-after speakers. She is also the founder and host of Women Thrive Summit - one of the largest global virtual women's empowerment events. Raimonda's passion is hosting events and helping other women become speakers and share their stories with the world. Her passion for speaking and empowering others stems from her own personal experience of losing her voice, her identity and confidence due to trauma, now that she has overcome her own life challenges and found the power in her voice she wants to make sure that no other woman has to hide her light and shy away from speaking up and sharing her story.

Your story matters and the world needs to hear about it.

www.raimondajankunaite.com
www.womenthrivesummit.com

2

THE UNTOLD STORIES

This chapter is dedicated to an unnamed woman whose story remains untold within these pages. Her silence is not a choice, but a consequence of legal constraints and power dynamics. This dedication extends to every woman facing similar struggles, unable to share her truth because of the fear of reprisals. It is a tribute to those whose voices have been silenced by the very forces that should empower them. In unity, we acknowledge the impact of fear and silence on women, and we stand against these forces that seek to disempower us.

It is a call to action, urging us to challenge the systems that muzzle voices, dismantle the structures that breed silence, and support one another in breaking free from these constraints.

In dedicating this page to the unheard, we also celebrate their resilience and strength. Despite the constraints, their spirits remain unbroken, and their stories, though unspoken here, echo in the collective heartbeat of countless others. We honour their courage, their tenacity, and their determination to reclaim their voices.

May this dedication serve as a beacon of hope for every

silenced woman, a testament to the solidarity that binds us together. Let it be a catalyst for change, inspiring us to create a world where every woman is free to speak her truth without fear, where her story is not just heard, but valued and respected.

3

YOU CAN HAVE IT ALL

BY POLI SEVCIKOVA

Anxieties shaped me, they changed me in ways I still discover. It's only a not-so-pleasant feeling in your body, so isn't this phrase just a tiny bit exaggerated?

20 years.

Of waves and waves of paralyzing fear rushing through your body and all the effects of that. Vomiting, every single day. Because the waves of fear were so many, so unstoppable, that my body could do only that. Vomit everything out. And feel relieved, at least for a few minutes.

This constant suffering, which you have seemingly no control over, does a lot to your body and mind.

Anxieties turned my world upside down, so I could throw out all the classic and 'normal' concepts of life from my mind and body.

They starved me for the desire for peace and happiness and gave me proof that absolutely nothing, NOTHING, is more important. Because truly, deeply, what can be more important, than breathing, smiling and not suffering?

For most of my life, I've felt so very abnormal.

I would go to school and most days end up throwing up due

to my feeling of anxiety, because of the waves that were constantly rushing through my body and wouldn't let me live in peace. It wouldn't let me live a normal life, like eating, sleeping, or enjoying school like most people. It was ever-present throughout my elementary, middle, high school, and university. I even contemplated the possibility of ending it. Death seemed much easier than taking another step forward and having to face this ordeal on a daily basis.

For 20 years, I thought I was the worst coward in the world. I couldn't understand the constant fear of everybody and everything. How else could you describe the never-ending inner battle for each and every step in the morning to go to school, to go on a date, to see a friend, or to kiss a boy? I often felt like giving up. I often felt like my life had no meaning because the constant inner battle was often just too much to face.

I was observing everybody else, enjoying their lives, almost never fearing anything and so wanting to experience a normal life too. To experience something so simple, that most of the people around me took for granted. Normal life. Breathing air without the fear of dying. Smiling at your beloved one, taking his hand. Going for a walk with your dog. Waking up and having a calm breakfast. Planning a trip with your bestie. Going to a coffee shop with your mum and then doing some shopping.

So ordinary for most people, who have never experienced anxiety...Not for me. For me, it was everything I craved, only to live that ordinary, normal day-to-day life, nothing fancy. Yet day in and day out I would be crippled by fear - what if...

What if I feel sick and can't go home?

What if they see that I'm panicking for no reason?

What if they see me being sick?

Luckily, the phrase 'Everything happens for a reason' kept me going. Because it means that my struggle was there for a reason. I was afraid but really stubborn, to find a way out. To find a cure, a miracle, anything.

But there was never a cure. That one miracle that would help me feel better.

It was a journey. One step forward and two steps back as I often retraumatized myself by pushing too far and fighting for my life.

Thanks to my stubbornness, over these 20 years, many changes in my life happened and the prison of my mind wasn't there anymore. Step by step, it got better and better. A lot of things helped. Therapies for sure. But also, many things that I can do by myself. I still love and use mindfulness techniques which keep my brain free from thoughts and 'movies' that often create fear. I love homeopathy and EFT, which work like magic not only for myself but also for my kids. Just any little work, that brings me back to my body, to the here and now, works.

The one thing that changed the chemistry in my body and helped me so much to... Motherhood.

That is why we are here.

My motherhood changed my mind in such a strange and unwavering way, that everything else felt like childsplay.

Just for a second, I could finally have it all. I had it all. A loving and supportive husband Michael, a healthy happy daughter Emma, and a smart creative mind that allowed me to earn money and provide for my family. My mind was bent by so much struggle in the previous years and now it was transformed by motherhood.

Unexpected change in how I felt, and in how I was thinking, led me to the one and only possible realization. I am a mother. I want to be an amazing mother, a present mother and an accomplished mother. I never wanted to be a mother who was tired and not able to be present because of her own suffering. I was so afraid that I would resent my children and husband, for giving up on my dreams because of them.

No way.

As a mother, all I wanted was to be a positive example for my daughter and show her that women can in fact have it all. A successful and present mother, a family that spends time together, travels, and explores the world and at the same time, each of the family members follows their own dreams and talents.

I found the power within me, to create what I love. It all fled out. All the ideas for projects, all the energy to learn everything from top to bottom. It felt like a Big Bang, it exploded in creation...for what felt like minutes, days, I started to build my own business, then another one, then another one. They were all connected, all were loved and cherished. But it was too much, too fast for me to handle. Too much, too fast, that I lost myself in the hustle, in the 'musts' in the 'to-do's' of each and every one of the projects.

But this is me, already giving you a little heads-up. Let's go to the story itself, let's dive into the crack of time and see what the universe planned for me. Because this is it, the experience that led me to where I stand now. That experience that helps me every day to support my clients on their journey. Without it, who knows?

The bad things, the good things, everything happens for a reason.

Whoa, I'm a Superwoman

I don't even get it, how come I'm not cracking? Normally - understand - in my 'normality', even the slightest amount of stress causes panic attacks for months. Months that feel like years. Times when I'm paralyzed with fear, can´t eat and feel the life going around me, feeling so alone. But this new me, with other ways to function is still really uncharted territory for me. My brain and body work differently than they did before I became a mum.

I really changed. I finally can live. Do what makes my heart sing and be a mum of this amazing little girl. Sometimes I still can't believe that. I never believed I could live such a normal life. But here I am. My hell gave me the strength I never imagined I'd have. I feel like a Superwoman.

That feels amazing. I feel the fire deep inside. The fire, that for decades was dimmed by the necessity to survive, is now burning bright. For my daughter, I will do anything.

Suddenly the fears that crippled me aren't important. For the first time in my life, I truly believe I can have it all. Build the businesses and projects of my deepest desire and have an amazing family life too. That's my vision. That's my goal. This is what I´m manifesting with my entire heart. Every day I feel into that vision, I listen to my intuition, and I say yes to things that excite me, even if they also scare me.

This powerful, deeply-felt vision is what created everything in the year to come. The universe got a clear message. She wants to have it all.

That's the part we all fear. The part when you go towards your dreams, do everything right, but suddenly your reality crumbles and nothing makes sense. The part when every experience and event is given to us, so we can start living that vision. It's all being created for us. But at that moment, we can't see it.

Because to live our vision, we sometimes need to first live through some experience. And, sometimes, like in my case, the experiences can get really rough. But they were meant to happen. For me to live it, and learn that really everything happens for us.

As a Business Architect who combines energy work with strategy, this is what I encounter almost on a daily basis with my clients. I support them in creating and holding their biggest vision, their version of 'having it all' and sometimes there is the part when it feels like nothing is working, and everything is crumbling…but if we stay in the vision, if we zoom out, we can see. Oh yes, we can see that it´s not really crumbling, it's creating a new reality that is happening.

A day of a Superwoman

From the time Emma was born, in the space of 2 years, between breastfeeding, and having no babysitting or money, I built several businesses. I love them all, they are amazing and in complete alignment with what I wanted to bring to this world.

The less pleasant part is that I have to switch between the 3 businesses quite a lot and I feel like juggling a million things at the same time. I run a community center for mothers and children, an e-shop with wooden toys, and a language school.

I usually wake up at 6 am and drive to a nearby storage, to pack all the orders of toys for that day to send.

Then I come back home, enjoy my breakfast with Emma and my husband Michael, and drive her to preschool. Emma started preschool just a few months back and luckily she really likes it there. My heart can rest and I can go on with my work schedule and Michael with his.

I teach Montessori and English lessons in my community center during the day.

When needed, I switch to teacher training for my language school.

And of course, let's not forget the packages that were prepared at 6 a.m., and need to be sent before I pick up Emma.

In my spare minutes, when I'm alone, I'm promoting all the projects, creating marketing strategies, communicating with my teams of teachers, doing some accounting, and well…you can imagine, just everything.

We have a mortgage now and all the responsibilities from my projects, so as a mother and a provider, I must do what it takes to take care of my family. Luckily, I love every little part of it, and the freedom that my work gives me. The 6 hours per day when Emma is in preschool, I get to run my businesses and do the things I love doing. That's just heaven, even if it's a really hasty heaven.

I hear from everybody that it's normal that in the first years of business, you need to hustle and it's totally ok that you work almost for free. I do it without even thinking there could be another way. If I persevere, my business will reward me in the years after with an overflow of money.

I bet you can already feel it. Maybe you are even living it right now. The Superwoman mother business owner's day-to-day hustle. The beliefs about business that are all around us, all the time. Hustle babe and then get rewarded. You can't ever have it all, you always need to sacrifice something. Sometimes time with your kids, sometimes sleep. You need to keep going and it will change by itself in a few years. I felt there was another way, and I was trying my very best to find it. I was already creating only things that lit me up, I was creating my businesses around my life, without the need to sacrifice time with my loved ones. But there were still many things that just weren't working. I still wasn't earning money, experiencing feelings of safety and calmness, and freedom flew out of the window too.

Luckily, there was the universe watching my back and saying - Little girl, you have your vision, and this won't get you to it. I am here to help you, to deliver your vision, so let's get to work, shall we?

First hit - my body

I am working every spare minute I get, loving what I do, and feeling the alignment helps me ignore my tiredness and my stress levels. There is no way out and I'm not even searching for it, because this is what business ownership looks like, am I right? I see it all the time. Our friends hustle, my husband hustles, so I do too.

It's the second half of January. It's freezing outside, with ice everywhere. I just went to the office in the city to finalize the paperwork for our grant submission. I squeezed this task into the only 30 minutes I had to spare in the morning. I don't even feel how stressed I am because of all the different tasks. I´m rushing towards my car, texting. I have 15 minutes to go back to the city and rush into my Montessori lesson. Blissfully unaware there is a thick layer of ice underneath my feet. One sudden, careless move and I find myself on the floor. As I fell to the ground, I could feel that my knee was in severe pain and it made me scream.

As I lay on the ground I feel so helpless, that one split second just changed everything. Thoughts rush through my mind, as I think about my clients probably already gathering for their Montessori lesson at my community center.

"I must be in my lesson within 15 minutes," I think to myself. "My clients with their babies are already on the way. There is nobody to take care of them. This can't be happening."

Only after a few seconds, did I realize the big picture. It's not only about arriving on time for this one morning lesson. I can't even stand up. I´m still lying on the ice. I can't even get back home, because I have our only car here, standing still right next to my head.

It took almost 10 minutes until somebody heard me, and carried me back inside the building.

As I was sitting there, surrounded by strangers in a lobby, I called my husband Michael and he took me to the hospital.

The doctor's diagnosis was clear. I have dislocated my knee and I was advised not to move for a month, as a minimum.

Due to my injury and inability to keep on going at the same pace as I was, the entire community center that I have built has had to go. Everything I built over the last 2 years. Surprisingly, I felt so relieved. No sadness, no remorse. I felt happy! In that moment, the injury felt like a blessing in disguise.

"What's happening?" I asked myself. This was my soul's purpose, how come I´m so ok with leaving it behind?

Instead of sadness, I felt excitement.

At this stage, I did not have my wooden toys e-shop anymore, because just a few weeks previously I gave it to my colleague. My language school can be led online because I´m not the one teaching the clients, as I have staff who can take over.

I'm supposed to take over my mother's lessons in a big company - 3 times per week for 8 hours - but I can do it even with my leg being injured. I already promised her months ago, to take over, because she had to go through a planned complicated surgery and wouldn't be able to teach her lessons. Because I teach Russian as she does, her clients know me and I needed the money, it was a no-brainer for both of us.

Whoa, how my life changed. In a blink.

This really helped. It freed up my calendar so much and got me ready to take over the teaching job from my mother, which offered me really good pay. "Ahh." I always craved that feeling of stability. Knowing that after I do what I´m good at, in a given time range, I will get paid and then I can go on with my day and just enjoy the time with my family. It was a relief knowing that I could let go of all the other jobs I had on my plate and finally bring in better money. At this point, I was pretty much the sole provider because my husband was still in the hustle-then-get-rewarded mode. So he was bringing money home, but not steadily, and often just not enough to sustain a family of 3 with a mortgage.

So in February, as my husband Michael was driving I felt a

deep need to tell him something. A big realization that was brewing within me in these last few days, as I was teaching and living a completely different life than before the accident. As I was enjoying that "Ahh" feeling of safety and calm.

"My love, we can´t get back to life before the accident. To me hustling without a paycheck. Now the lessons in the company showed us how nice it feels when regular money flows in but it will end shortly. Plus, my other businesses are still too young to bring money."

So I pronounce something I thought I would never ever say.

"Michael, I feel we need to find me a job."

Why was it so unthinkable for me? Working given hours, closed in an office when I can't leave even a second earlier, was the same as going back to school and not being able to go away. Meaning, that even thinking of having a job was causing me the same anxieties and panic attacks as before I became a mum. And also, it always felt that it would be like giving up on my dreams, giving up on my freedom, and becoming a tired robot.

But the experience of money stability shifted those feelings a little bit. Not entirely, but it opened my head to the slight possibility that I could find a way to work, earn steady money, and not go back to crushing panic attacks.

Phew, it's out there and I feel relieved that I shared that revelation with my husband. I already know that this is my sign, that I did the right thing. I´m capable and smart, I will find something that will make sense to me and my priorities. On the other hand, I can work only a few hours per day, because I need to take care of Emma and my other projects, plus my anxieties didn't disappear, so I know I can't be closed up in an office. Will I even find something? All these thoughts were rushing through my head as we were driving.

We called our headhunter friend and had a deep talk with him about my possibilities in the job market with regard to all of the factors. The only ideal option he could suggest, was for me to learn PPC ads (Pay per click ads on Google). This will let me work remotely, on any schedule and it's paid well too. This way, I can take care of our daughter as needed and still earn good money.

Did I get lucky and magically find work as a Junior who wanted to learn how to do ads? No. I did the work, I Googled a lot. I wrote many emails. I got on several meetings and, after all of that, I found a great mentor at a company that led me to work from home. So I started learning about PPC ads on Google, evening breaks between lessons and weekends. In just a few months, I was earning amazing money and still had a ton of time for my language school, which I kept, because I led it remotely, as I wasn't the one teaching our clients. And guess what, with 2 of my friends we got European funding to build a brand new, private Montessori preschool! We had hoped for this for almost a year.

It felt like a dream come true. $200k to build a unique preschool for our children and for our community, that knew me well already from the community center. I can continue with creating projects that I love for myself, and for my daughter, and this time, with funding.

But the universe wasn't really done with me. Why?

PPC ads in another company, non-stop work on the preschool. So, I'm doing the hustle again, without realizing it.

I now had the money for my family and I was building what I love, so it seemed like my vision and all I wanted were already there. But I was still working my ass off by switching between businesses and family, never finding the time for myself to recharge. My capability of filling any free time with work was really admirable, but it was only my childhood trauma hitting me in a new way.

Instead of panic attacks, I was becoming a workaholic mom who was forgetting about herself. Why? Because the only way to survive anxieties for me was to think of something else, do something else, something that would keep my mind occupied at all times. This way my head wouldn't have the time to think of any fear and cause me a panic attack. Here it was, my pattern of survival created in all these years. Studying, reading, watching movies, just anything. This time, it was creating a business from scratch.

So, Although it seemed from the outside like I was successful and I felt successful as well, I really did not have it all. No one, and especially not me, could tell I was going towards burnout really fast.

Second hit - my heart

I was lost and I didn´t know about it. So the universe wheeled out the big guns in order that I would remember what life is all about and return to my priorities.

I still feel like it was yesterday. One second, she is a vibrant 92-year-old woman. Calling me once in a while, stopping by with a bag full of groceries just because she loves to spoil me, chit-chattin' about everything and nothing while drinking tea and looking at Emma, as she is playing around us.

But then one day, when she came to visit me again, I saw that her skin was yellow.

We hadn't seen each other for just a week. I asked her if the yellow skin is from today?

"No my dear, I've been yellow for several days now, but it's ok. I feel alright and I definitely won't go to any doctor!" Oh yes, classical grandma. She was a war nurse and a midwife, after the war. For more than 20 years, she was an ICU emergency nurse in Saint Petersburg. She only self medicated, hated to listen to the instructions of doctors.

"Lipa, we need to go! Let's go right away to the hospital." She wasn't happy about it, but I saw in her eyes that she was worried too, and I was the only one she listened to.

After several hours in the hospital and many different tests, Lipa had surgery. But after the surgery, I got the news that nobody is ever prepared for.

"It's incurable. We can't help her. It will take a few days or maybe weeks, but you need to get ready for the fact that it's terminal," the doctor said.

In another month, May to be exact, I was burying her. I was with her 'til the last breath. Holding her hand, smiling at her in the moments she couldn't move anymore. I fought for her, so she could have these last days at home, and I am so grateful I was able to give her that.

She was never only my grandma. She practically raised me. She was the one I am most similar to, she was the only one I could tell anything. She always told me, "Don´t cry my love, you are stronger than this." And now? I can´t stop crying. You know that one thing you fear for years, that sometime it might come? This was it for me. I knew, I always knew, that if something happened with Lipa, it would destroy me. And it did. Completely, deeply and forever.

I cried for days. Sometimes feeling that I will never be able to stop crying.

I couldn't seem to find a single reason to smile anymore. A single reason to even bother to be happy. How could I? When she's not here? How could I care about some client, Google Ads, grant, even that photoshoot for a magazine. How could I care about my husband, again, not being able to sustain us? Making me work even while planning the funeral?

I was a living zombie. Just working and taking care of my child. No smile, just courtesy. Crying whenever I was alone. No motivation to look forward, just taking one step at a time. Surviving in the best way I could.

This was a really low blow for me. And I still haven't gotten completely over it. I cry even writing about it, talking about it, thinking about it.

I understand why. Of course. I have gotten off alignment. I forgot what is important. Even if just slightly, I derailed. Now I remembered what was important. Only health and love. Nothing else. Other things can be replaced, regrown, and rebuilt... but we have only one life, only one body and soul. We have only the NOW to be with our loved ones, not some days in the future that really aren't guaranteed. We have only one body, so escaping from it all the time isn't the way.

I feel it, deep there, changing the way I see myself, my marriage, and my day-to-day life.

Third hit - my marriage

The death of my beloved grandma Lipa changed me, but I wasn't living my life alone. My life was affected by my husband too. And he was still pushing up the old way. The hustle, the sacrifice. And I felt it, saw it like I never saw it before.

I was blind and now I could see it clearly.

Even if I was a living zombie. On the contrary, my state helped me to see some things much clearer. And because I was so utterly emotionally exhausted, I was much less reluctant to bullshit and waste any more precious time in our life.

So I saw how my husband lived in the hope that one day things would change.

He is completely okay with me cutting loose my companies, learning new things, and giving our family stability, but he wasn't doing the same. He was trying. Of course. He was doing his best. Yes. But he continued to hope for this one road to finally kick in, and give us the wealth he wanted. 3 years. 3 years of him not being home with us, earning money from time to time, putting us in financial crisis over and over again. This is the harsh reality of striving for your dreams and short-term sacrifices over long-term dreams.

I let him work towards his vision and always have been

supportive, but after 3 years we had to do something. I needed to be able to lean on my man, not only emotionally because that was never our problem, but also financially. I need my husband present with our family, not only in hopes for the future but in real day-to-day life, because I was too exhausted to carry it all on my own. I felt alone. And I didn't feel safe, or secure, which caused lots of stress in my body. I needed to feel this, for the sake of me and my daughter.

It was a total nightmare, even thinking about this, but saying it out loud?! But I had to do it so we could be financially stable and finally have some space to breathe, without worrying all the time.

So one evening, after I put Emma to sleep I told Michael we needed to talk. I knew one thing. I must be harsh, I must be even cruel. Or he won't hear me. He won't understand it completely. He will just forget about it, like so many times before, and go on with it, like always. This I knew from our 14 years together.

"Michael, I can't support you any longer in any way. You planned your way to the top, and for 3 years you dragged us through it with you. Emma doesn't even want to hug you anymore. I don't want you to touch me anymore, either. I only pay the bills and work. And from you, I hear only some hopes about the next month being better. But look at the reality. It's never better. Ever. I let go of everything. Now you need to do the same. To wake up and start working somewhere with a regular paycheck. Or, I will walk away. It will break my heart, but if there is no other way for you to see it, I will do it." I was upset and I felt like we reached the end of the road with the way our life was going. It was a moment that was going to make or break us.

I saw in Michael's eyes the immense shock after realizing what he was doing to our family. The part he played in our crushed dreams and how it was affecting everyone around him.

He crashed and crumbled from the notion of me and Emma walking away and that transformed him. A little bit. He needed some more kicks too, to change not only his life but our life altogether.

Fourth hit - my baby(ies)

We started to implement the changes. Michael found a paid job with the potential to grow. And I was building my preschool while leading my language school and earning most of our money as a marketing strategist and PPC ads manager.

Since my grandma died, I felt this totally unbelievable feeling, that somebody was coming.

We frankly didn't plan to have more children. We still weren't financially okay, and our marriage was so fragile in these summer months.

But that feeling was there.

And then September 2017 was here.

I feel so sick, all day, every day.

Hmmm, it feels somewhat similar to when I was pregnant with Emma. I thought to myself.

So one evening, just for fun, I did a pregnancy test. I wasn't expecting it to be positive. No freaking way!

I can't be pregnant now! We are opening our preschool, I'm feeding our family and Michael is away all the time in his new job!

Ok, breathe.

There is nothing I can do, so I will do my best to survive these first few months.

Breathe.

My paid job as a PPC specialist can be done from bed, as can my language school.

My hopes were one thing, but the reality of the next few days was quite different.

I really can't work. My brain isn't working with all the nausea and I can't eat at all.

But there's nothing I can do. I don't see any way out.

One afternoon I went with Emma and our friends to a playground.

Chatting, playing, laughing.

I needed this time off SO much. Amazing normal afternoon.

One minute, I hear our children laughing, and running, and then, suddenly, I hear Emma screaming her lungs out.

I turned my back for a second and didn't see it happening.

She is sitting on the floor and holding her hand in a weird way. Shit. I need to take her to the hospital.

I hug her, kiss her, and try to calm her down a little bit. My friend hangs my bag on my shoulder and just says - “Go!”

So I go. I carry her quickly to our car and to the emergency.

Because I am pregnant, I can´t hold her while she is getting an X-ray. This can't be happening.

I see her through a glass, so scared, in pain, crying, alone. Oh my baby, not you, not now.

While we were waiting for the results, I called Michael and told him what happened, crying on the phone. He is in Prague, but coming back home to us as fast as he can.

Emma´s hand is broken. She won’t be able to attend preschool for a month.

Me, pregnant, sick all the time. This is the last part of my husband’s transformation that our family needed.

That day, he came home and stayed. He chose us. I admire him for this so much, and never will stop admiring him. Because he has made this choice every day, all these years, since that first time.

He left everything he had known and stayed home with me and Emma . And we never looked back.

The strangest thing is, that the solution to all of our problems is suddenly so obvious.

I taught him everything about marketing and Google Ads. We even arranged it in such a way that he could take my place in the prestigious marketing studies that I just got in.

Thanks to all of this, he will, in a matter of a few months, switch with me in the marketing agency, take my clients, and give us financial stability - instead of me.

Right from the start of this plan, I felt the big pressure leaving my shoulders. I can carry our second child and finally, for the first time in my life, feel safe and secure. Feel taken care of and loved.

We have even started to plan our first family vacation! We finally have a stable regular money stream and freedom to go whenever we want to. So it's decided, we are going to Poland for a week.

I am still very sick and tired all the time and that motivates us to get away from all that stress of the new preschool, as fast as possible.

My promises

Oh yes, when you think your dreams have come true, but the universe isn't done with you just yet.

It's late October 2017, our first-ever family vacation. We are enjoying the beautiful Gdansk in Poland. Exploring, relaxing.

Then one night...

"Why am I living, what's the point of it? Might it be easier to just go out to the balcony and jump?"

it was a second, maybe just a mili-second, that crossed my mind, but still the thought came.

It emerged in the dark of the night, just like it did so many times before in my life, all tied up to a panic attack.

But at this moment, it was different. I really didn't expect it. I am different, and still, here it is, again. What the hell?

Michael took most of the work from my shoulders, I'm leading 'only' the preschool and the language school.

I just can't feel like this. This is not happening. I'm definitely not feeling the waves of anxiety coming through my body.

Behind the wall, my husband Michael and Emma are sleeping. And even thinking of them, makes the anxiety even stronger.

I´m finally living my dream, how come I feel like I'm dying?

Deep down, I know the answer. I feel it there for quite a while, but I am fighting it, repressing it, ignoring it right up to the point when it bursts in the form of an unexpected panic attack during my vacation.

Shit.

The preschool.

We built it with 2 of my friends, these last 6 months, and everything around it is causing me burnout. I feel sick just by looking at the missed calls on my phone. And even the daily 'pregnancy' sickness went away after we arrived in Poland. That can't be a coincidence.

I thought that I was already trained in letting go after this year, but I am still clinging to it.

Because I have an obligation, many obligations in the preschool. I made a promise of what will be my responsibility when we were first applying for the grant. I am the marketer, the leader, the director. I am the one holding the vision and leading us towards it. I am the glue between us three.

I need to stay in kindergarten because of my 2 colleagues. We built this dream preschool from thin air, just for our children and our community. I can't just leave them. These were the thoughts rushing through my mind.

But, my body and mind think otherwise. This idea of

jumping off the balcony is one of the last signals I needed to reevaluate my life again.

After returning from Poland, I managed it for a few more days. All the phone calls, meetings, stress, at the same time taking care of Emma, taking care of my last marketing clients...but my underbelly started to hurt. Last straw.

It took all the courage I had left. My rediscovered priorities kept me going, remember those? The health and happiness of my family and mine. Everything else...well everything else can change, even if it breaks my heart.

I talked about it for hours with Michael. He saw me suffering, but he knew that the impulse to leave the preschool couldn't come from him. But when it came from me, he agreed.

Now I just need to find the right time to do it.

It was decided that I am really doing it, leaving the preschool, leaving it to my other 2 partners and friends to run it.

So the day came. In kindergarten, we had our first Halloween party with kids and their parents. We all went wild and had a lot of fun. When everyone left only the three of us, the owners, remained with our children. Cleaning, chatting...I knew that the moment had come.

I'm taking a big breath in, big breath out. I feel my voice and legs shaking as I ask the girls to take a break because I need to talk to them.

I shared with them my last months, as I've done with you, especially how I was physically unwell in these last weeks, and how it was starting to endanger the baby. I saw the understanding in their eyes. They are mothers too, they know that nothing is more important than the health of our children.

We cried a lot. And that was it. They didn't scream at me, they didn't feel betrayed by me, they didn't stop loving me. They embraced me. They understood me. I never felt so loved by another friend as I did that day.

I always thought that leaving means that that person won't ever talk to me again. That thinking of my health and myself is selfish and I just needed to push through it, ignore it as long as possible. I was afraid they would see me as weak if I left, if I stopped pushing.

As we hugged each other, these thoughts were suddenly erased. I understood, finally, after my entire life surrounded by these beliefs, that it's just bullshit, and nothing else.

I knew that from that moment on, I was just another mom in the preschool. Just their friend as before the preschool, no longer a sidekick, no longer a director. I left.

It didn't kill me. On the contrary, there was a huge sense of relief, but also a lot of sadness and a sense of failure.

How come you left the preschool you prayed for and built in the sweat of your face?!

Loss in my ego's eyes. All the losses of this last year came back rushing in. I lost so much. I left so many of my creations behind, I lost. I felt like a failure. Because in my mind's perception, when you leave something, it's a failure.

I left my e-shop, my community center, my preschool. I lost my grandma. I almost lost my husband. I wasn't there for my daughter in her scariest moment. How much can a little girl like me survive? I have nothing more to give or to leave. Suddenly I don't have anything to do. No goal to struggle for. No battle to fight. No fear to overcome. No things that would show me I am good enough. But this is my mind talking. The never-ending battle of the ego and self-worth attached to doing, being, and having to strive for more.

My heart and body are feeling completely different. My heart says that this was the only possible right step. The relief is very deep, very strong. Even the emptiness that my mind was fearing, my body needed this relief and, finally, rest. I stopped and it was ok.

That sense of absolute freedom and peace. Something I've never known.

And the funny thing is that the void, in just one month, brought a new project, a marketing agency of our own, a business that we started building together with my husband right away, just a few months before our son was born. That was the beginning of a new life that we have been creating ever since. The vision, that I mentioned before we dove into this year, started to become a reality. In ways we could never plan, or imagine.

Life when we are together at home. We have a lot of time for our children, for ourselves. We live and work, but none of the parts drain us anymore.

I can have it all. We all can have it all.

Trauma can sense trauma

6 years later and we are still living our dream. The dream that I saw in the vision and felt in my body - I can have it all. I see that for it to become a reality, we needed to live through those tough experiences. Without them, we couldn´t further evolve our vision, as we are doing now.

The good in the bad had not only short-term change results but mostly long-term ones.

"6 years later and this one year is still living in me. It's there to guide me. To check on me."

How? You might ask?

My body experienced such intense emotions in that year, the death, the burnout, the loss, the despair, that it created a system of control that lets me know when I´m going towards some other extreme. For example, I fill my calendar too much with clients, rush towards new goals too fast, follow 'go-to' methods instead of my inner guidance, or push myself too much in any other part of my internal or external work.

And I just know that nothing, NOTHING, is more important. Only health, love, happiness, and peace. This helps me to continuously adjust, and harmonize any part that calls for change within or around me. To slow down, recharge. When my love towards my business goes too far, I go to my secret nook in the house and just read. As an introvert, when I spend too much time around people, I get tired and I need to recharge. Then, I send the kids to my mum or my mother-in-law, book a hotel and enjoy time with my husband, so we can have some time to ourselves to recharge.

I like this kind of inner stubbornness, it gives me strength and often patience to take the time with the changes. My heart says - "you can always find a way, because you survived so much worse. You can have it all and you will, on your terms, without any sacrifices."

Over the years of struggle, I learned the art of harmonizing my life, and designing my business around my life and priorities. Thanks to that, I can do the same with my clients as well which helps them alleviate the struggle. The true magical thing is being able to combine energy and strategy, which works so much better than just strategy alone. Thanks to all the challenges that I lived through, I can see the traumas playing in the lives of my clients and I can support them to overcome them, so they can truly build something, that is coming from their deepest desires and gifts. I hold the space for their highest version so it can be created, so they can see it, feel it, and go towards it.

In these last years, I have helped thousands of women, to stop the vicious circle before they burned out, redesign their businesses before it was too late, and design their business as a support system for themselves in the first place. We design their businesses from the beginning with the presumption that they can have it all and that there is no need to sacrifice anything, just to be smart about it - exactly as I do - and be in alignment with their heart.

Thanks to this approach, we always design the business around the unique life priorities and talents of each of my clients. We don't ever presume that there is just one way to build a business or design your 'successful' life. Success is what feels good on the inside and not just what looks good from the outside.

I don't believe in go-to methods, strategies or anything else. We are all individuals. Forged in the depths of our traumas, shining with our heart's calling and gifts.

We can all have it all.

It is there for us to claim, as long as we decide to follow our heart instead of some outer guidance.

When we live through certain life events and overcome trauma, we can identify it in another person much sooner. We can sense it with our 6th sense. This is just a simple fact and something I learned through my extensive training as an energy healer. Because when we are healed, we can see the pain but our own trauma isn't switching on or triggered. That's why it is so important to go on our healing journey, because otherwise trauma can switch on a trauma in another human. Because trauma recognizes trauma.

Today, this helps me so much in my work. Because often, everything in my client's business is designed perfectly, the next launch is planned, the team is working amazingly but the sales are just not coming through, people aren't reacting or even ads aren't working as they are supposed to. There is no logical reason why this should be happening. I can sense it with my body, that there is a trauma, and this way, we can start not only to heal it, but also be more gentle with the nervous system of the client and create everything in such a way that they can grow, steadily, long-term, without retraumatizing herself. We figure out what the blessing was in such a phase, where something wasn't working without any logical reason, and from that place my clients always grow immensely. They need to go through the experience, even if it's not a desirable one, to come to the realisation experience on themselves, that everything is being created for them, including the 'unpleasant' things in their business or life.

Being me, I feel when some strategies, pricing, or packaging, puts our bodies in such distress that, instead of giving us freedom, they stress us so much that we go into overload. And if we don´t stop in time, burnout is just around the corner.

A new way of doing business

Most often, it's not about what we do, but HOW we do it and HOW WE FEEL, that allows us to create a new way of doing business that feels at ease.

6 years ago, I was checking the alignment of WHAT I was doing, building, creating, and because I knew the projects were the right ones, I kept going.

But I couldn't see that I lost myself in HOW to do it. Because that matters sometimes even more. How we divide our time, attention and money matters. Should we push ourselves, spend all the time and money towards one project with the vision that it would be better in the future? Is that the best way to do it? I can tell you now, that we can be more smart about it. A business will always take what we give to it. But as mothers, we often just don't have the luxury to lose ourselves in our business, nor do we want that to happen, am I right? Sometimes it's so easy to do that. Business gives us a sense of purpose, we love working with our clients, creating new opportunities, new projects, earn money. But other times, our kids stop us. It's harder to work when our kid is at home sick. And if we take this into account while designing our business in the first place, the business can support us and doesn't crumble if we don't give it 100% attention for a few days or even weeks. That's an important choice and not always the easy one and the visible one right away. But it matters in the long run and I believe that you, like me, are all in it for the long run, for stable growth and harmony in life.

Another part about the HOW is the fact that the notion of Female Designed business is actually really new. Because there were never so many women in human history that had the possibility to build their own businesses and have a fulfilling family life as well.

And that´s the reason why the HOW we build our business can sometimes feel hard for us. We could build a business as men, but we don't have the same body; the female body has monthly rhythms, and a different mind to a man's. So here I am, sharing my lesson, that cost me almost everything to figure it out.

You can choose. Forget about all the DOs and DON'Ts in business design, and create it around yourself. I am here to support you all the way.

There are millions of ways to build a business. There are millions of ways to be happy and successful, to have it all, without the need to sacrifice anything from our vision of a rich life. So where do we start?

I created a journey towards our uniquely crafted business design in these last few years, where I take you through energy work, where we connect you to your inner wisdom and then we create smart and effective strategies with the help of your heart. But most of my clients start with discovering their Success Matrix archetype. Thanks to that, we can start plugging into what success and a rich life means to us as individuals, and what our soul came here to create.

Success Matrix Archetypes are one of the most magical things I channeled. They came to me, after I asked my heart - ok, I can build whatever business with my clients. We have the energy work, the healing and the strategy, but how do we know what type of business or even business model to start with?

In that moment, the Archetypes came rushing in. They appeared in my head, for me to never forget them. They always show my clients which road is their own, which road is theirs to take. The one of an Adventurer or a Luxury Queen? Or maybe a Lazy Rebel like me and a Future builder? We have 8 archetypes and if you want to you can find out which one is the most powerful in you, just check the link in my bio and take the quiz.

Find the blessing in the hard

Last but not least. In these last 6 years, I built a marketing agency, a female entrepreneur platform and, most importantly, I've been a mentor for more than 4 years.

That was the funniest thing. When I was creating and leaving my projects a little voice in my head loved to tell me that I was crazy to build so many amazing projects and, with no regret, at some point in time, often leaving them to my colleagues; as I did with my language school, my Montessori preschool and my marketing agency.

Only after learning more about energy work, did I find out this...

We attract our reality with our emotions, with a clear vision and the universe serves. Everything is created for us, so we can have that reality from our vision. Only our mind doesn't know that, because she can create only from the known, she learns only from past experiences. But our intuition, our heart, is connected to our much wiser versions.

Thanks to that knowledge I came to the point where I saw that all those experiences were just the start of my real purpose. They were my experiences that needed to be lived. I needed to do it all, from top to bottom, so I could be the fantastic business architect that I am now. For you, for me.This is why my heart, at that moment, 6 years ago, was ok, when I left the preschool, while pregnant. My heart knew that everything was ok, everything was being created for me. My intuition saw much further than my ego could. This is why I felt so calm in the midst of all those things, even if the ego was screaming at me, that I can't just leave a business like this and go on with my life.

This is the most important part, if not anything else, take this from my story.

When it happens, the difficult thing often doesn't make sense. We feel it's all wrong, we don't deserve to suffer so much. Or the circumstances make us leave something we love, and we don't understand why we feel relieved, even if our head is screaming with discontent.

Believe me when I say this...

Time will show you what a blessing there was for you, in that difficult situation. Time will show you, that you maybe left the good, for the amazing, that is yet to come. Or maybe even if you zoom out and try to see the big picture, you will see it right away.

Because with our conscious mind, we can't foresee our future and control how exactly it will end up. We can only feel and see our vision, and let go of trying to control how it will be created in real life.

But our intuition, our heart, that's something completely different. The heart, the universe, or our Higher self (whatever you want to call it), can see further. It knows where we are headed. What we need to experience, let go, do - even if we feel we can't survive it.

I am a living proof of it and I bet you are too.

We often hear this saying - find the blessing within the heart. But without actual proof, it's just some phrase to calm us down in a moment of agony.

But, if made consciously, this effort to find the good in the bad can be the start of your healing, or the middle, or the end.

It doesn't matter, as long as you try living with this belief and looking at your day-to-day life through this lens. I do it.

So you know what, let's try it. Because there's no harm in trying, am I right? Write down what blessing you found in your bad experience, in the worst imaginable thing you went through. Where did it lead you? What did it give you? What did it wake within you?

I'm looking forward to getting to know you and start creating the life and business of your wildest dreams!

POLI SEVCIKOVA

Poli combines energy and strategy work because she truly believes one can't work without the other. As a former Facebook Ad Specialist and creator of 5 companies, she first tested everything on herself. And now, she helps other business owners design their unique businesses as well. She doesn't believe in the hustle and will always choose the way of more ease for her clients. Poli has faced many struggles with anxiety and panic attacks for her entire life. Every day, really every second of her life, she felt the monstrous weight of it, but she never let it define her. She never felt strong, but she knows who she is. If you tell Poli something can't be done, she will do it. She will play with it and find a way. This is why she loves so much what she does; she designs and builds businesses around the lives of her clients and around her life too. Because we deserve to have it all. When Poli isn't working, she is with her loving husband and her two children, celebrating 20 years together.

https://polisevcikova.com/linktree

4

WAKE-UP CALL

BY CHRISTELLE PILLOT

"Il va bien, le bébé?" (Is the baby doing well?)

I look at Adrian, his big green eyes, his gentle face, the pure naivety of my 3-year-old son. This phrase penetrates so easily in my mind... "Oh! he spoke to me in French, that's rare". I feel tears welling up. "Great!" Driving back home, I promised myself not to cry. I lasted two seconds... "Well done, Christelle". I can't contain my tears. Martin, my partner, and Adrian, both heading towards the bathroom to take a shower, look at me with curiosity and surprise. I turn my head and see Théo's blond head, peeking through the door; he was playing quietly in his room. My second little boy, 2 years and a week old, observes the scene without saying a word, as if he sensed that something was happening. Théo doesn't talk much but observes a lot.

I turn my head again and gaze into the blue eyes of my partner, "Es gibt kein Baby mehr..." (There is no baby anymore). My emotions overwhelm me, that infamous lump in my throat that hurts every time I try to suppress a complicated emotion. And my mind keeps repeating like a mantra, "but it's okay, it's nature, everything is fine..."

I can't speak anymore. Between sobs, I ask Martin for 30 minutes to collect myself. I close the door behind me and put myself into position. I inhale, exhale. My throat hurts... I focus and cling to my breath like a buoy. I inhale and exhale... and, as always, it calms down, my breathing transforms, becoming gentler, slower... I am so grateful that meditation has been part of my daily life for decades now. Once again, this technique saves me. Like a spectator, I see the emotions within me passing by:

Sadness: "okay, well, it's normal," I tell myself. "The little being that lived inside me will not come into the world, I believe that it is appropriate to feel sad..."

Surprise: I really didn't expect this news. Our first two children came into the family with so little complication that I was 100% sure it would be the same for number 3.

We had just returned from vacation, and had been back home in Frankfurt, Germany, since yesterday. It's true that I was very tired at the beginning of July but the sun, the sea of the south of France, a relaxed rhythm, I felt good.

And then again, I'm surprised by my reaction. "Why am I so sad?" Early miscarriages in the first trimester are so common that one in four women experiences them. My head understands it perfectly, but inside, I feel so empty, so sad... "Why am I so sad?" Maybe it's because we said that if it wasn't now, then it would be too late for the third child. I had just turned 35, Martin is 41. We both agreed on this limit.

"Oh! I feel no anger..." That makes me smile inwardly. I've been working intensively on my anger for the past three years, meditating it away and apparently I've reached a new level. "Congrats!"

I inhale, exhale, accept the present emotions, and let them pass. I'm calming down, start thinking about the coming days. I'm still on vacation for 2-3 more days, and then I'm going to Slovenia. I'm a chemical engineer, working for a French company, developing a distributor network internationally to sell our chromatography devices. On Monday, I'll be at a customer´s R&D lab in Croatia with the Slovenian distributor. But before Monday, I still need to arrange my hospital appointment for a curettage. I have to call right away; I need to act quickly.

I come out of my meditation, calm, and I start explaining the situation to Martin. I talk to the children. "Mom might be sad in the next few days, and Dad might be too, but it's okay and it's normal. Everything is fine. The baby decided not to come, but there must be a good reason for it. And you, you can continue to laugh and play. Is that okay for you?"

Grief

I land in Ljubljana. The weather is beautiful, my Slovenian colleague picks me up, and we head straight to the client's pharmaceutical research center. No one is aware of my little drama, and that's fine. My hands are covered in bruises. As usual, they had to try multiple times for the anesthesia injection, a real mess. My Slovenian colleague has seen it and asks questions. I joke, I deflect... and we focus on the blue machine in front of us and the client's questions, along with his team.

I look at the machine, lost in thought. It performs a beautiful separation of chemical compounds... It's simple with machines. No emotions. It's clear: they were built for a specific purpose, no confusion, no existential questions, no emotional overload or intrusive thoughts. The exact opposite of us humans, especially me, who increasingly asks myself, "But what am I doing here? What's the point of all this? What am I doing on this earth?" Ever find yourself pondering this mystery too?

I will stay in Ljubljana for three days. The days are spent discussing machines and, in the evenings, I tend to my sadness.

This late August feels like a dream, the city is filled with music. I stroll through the lively and joyful streets of Ljubljana. The sun's rays gently caress my skin. Passersby go about their activities, unaware of the sadness within me. Some songs are slow, tinged with nostalgia, and every word seems to touch my soul.

The lyrics reverberate within me, finding an echo in my own feelings. In this unfamiliar city, shielded by anonymity, I am overwhelmed by emotion and let my tears flow freely. The passersby still go about their activities, still unaware of my now visible sadness and, strangely, I feel reassured by that. I can really let go without having to justify myself or worrying about the emotions of someone else. I can properly say goodbye to my baby.

Every evening, I continue to wander through the streets. There is something comforting about this city. The combination of its serenity and the sadness that envelops me creates a strange sense of peace. Once again, I find myself surprised by the absence of anger, replaced instead by self-compassion and a gentle feeling. I like this new peaceful wisdom in me. On top of that, It feels as though the universe helped me by designing this place for my healing. The city's atmosphere couldn't have been more perfect.

I have always loved traveling alone and discovering new places. Over the last 15 years, my journeys led me to live in England, Germany, and China. It was during my stay in China, at a conference, that serendipity intervened and brought Martin into my world, at the time he was a young German PhD student. Here again, I have the feeling that the universe did its part in uniting us again later in Frankfurt.

Anyway, every time I arrive in a new place, I feel like I find myself again, as if I have the freedom to be who I truly am, as if I can upload a new version of myself or become whoever I want to be. It's a real breath of freedom for me. If you had the chance to start over, have you ever wondered who you might become?

What path would you choose, and what new version of yourself would you upload into the world? What kind of silly or unusual behavior would you adopt, just for fun?

Interestingly, when I was 30, I sought guidance from a therapist for my recurring bouts of depression. She suggested that my passion for traveling served as a form of self-therapy. Maybe she is right… Or is there a chance that, instead, I may have been using travel to escape from something?

Business as usual

Back home. This trip did me good, I am so glad I didn't cancel it. At home, things are back to normal. As if nothing had happened. Business as usual, family as usual. The children no longer think about last week. “That's good, so muss es sein” (That's good, that's how it should be) and Martin will certainly never mention that event again. 10 years later, I know he has an astonishing ability to manage these types of emotions with serenity and acceptance.

I'm answering my emails, feeling empty, but I believe it's okay: Time heals all wounds. Time and a quiet day at the office is exactly what I need. When I'm not traveling, I work from home, well home-office. My colleagues are in France or elsewhere. It's convenient to avoid talking about oneself.

In the weeks ahead, there are no trips planned, and the return to September feels surprisingly uneventful. It appears that my recent journey to Slovenia has faded from people's minds, as nobody has inquired about it. Similarly, my ongoing projects in Brazil, Japan, and India aren't sparking much interest within the company. All of this only serves to strengthen the persistent question in my mind: "What is the purpose of it all?"

I find myself putting in so much effort, tirelessly designing new business opportunities, navigating through different cultures and administrations, and persuading people both in France and abroad. It's a constant juggling act between my family and work, and it often feels like I'm sacrificing precious time while traveling. Sometimes, I even end up spending two consecutive nights on the plane, trying to shorten my stay abroad. These challenges make me wonder about the purpose of all this hard work. Maybe some see it as a strategic role for the company's future expansion, but right now, it all feels insignificant. Despite my appreciation for our machines, I'm not passionate about the company's ultimate goal: to grow and make more money. It feels like my existence revolves solely around generating profits. This thought leaves me weary and exhausted. I'm tired of it all.

This isn't the first time I've felt this lack of energy, this desire to do nothing. This impression that everything becomes too difficult. That it takes an insurmountable amount of energy to make a phone call or write an email. I've had these episodes since I was a teenager, and in recent years, they've become more frequent, closer together, and deeper. Short psychotherapy, a lot of personal development and years of meditation sessions have helped me understand many things, but the depressions are still there.

This one seems harder. I feel like I'm losing my grip. My willpower is no longer enough to do the bare minimum. Lately, for example, I pick up the kids at 6:00 PM and, honestly, if the daycare allowed it, I would pick them up at 8:00 PM and put them directly to bed. It's really absurd. I'm not the fun and energetic mom that these two children deserve and I am not the mom that I want to be for them. I also see my performance at work declining, and it's eating me up.

I'm someone who advocates for doing good work and tenacity but my energy is no longer enough for a full day. With a superhuman effort, I manage to do what needs to be done in the morning, but generally, I collapse around 1:00 PM. Once again, no one notices, but that doesn't comfort me either. I am disappointed in myself.

Not to mention my relationship with my husband, who doesn't understand me and doesn't see where the problem lies anyway. We're growing apart. He says I've lost my sense of humor and he doesn't want to hear my problems. I can't confide in anyone else. And honestly, I'm too ashamed... I've learned my lesson well, never show your weaknesses, "fake it until you make it". If you have weaknesses, you overcome them. Period. So, I'm alone with a family to take care of. I struggle with my lack of energy when there's so much to do, and I'm convinced that I am a loser, a fraud, and for now, no one sees it, but it will eventually come to light. Do you know what this feels like? You advocate for values that you no longer live by, you are completely out of alignment with the person you have become. You don't recognize yourself anymore. Your surroundings don't see any difference and continue to love and admire you for what you no longer are, which deepens the feeling of impostor syndrome, of loneliness, like living in a parallel world. I'm ashamed, I'm an impostor, I'm desperate, and this time I don't see a way out.

Escape

"I don't see a way out. I feel stuck..." I wanted to change countries, but it's not possible this time. I suggested Spain since Martin and I both speak enough Spanish to start over there and Barcelona is definitely one of my favorite cities. But Martin didn't like the idea. I don't have a new challenge to take on, which usually revitalizes me. I like challenges; they make me grow and learn things. They give me a sense of progress and accomplishment, like I'm moving towards something better....

A shiver runs down my spine. The baby... the baby was my escape. That's why I've been so sad since he's gone, and I can't seem to bounce back. I used the baby as a means to escape from my work, to flee the emptiness of my life. With the baby, I would have had a break of maybe six months, and I would have had more time and opportunity to rearrange my life, our life. How horrible, I feel disgusted. What kind of person am I to use a human being, the life of an innocent little human being, my baby, to escape from my problems? “What a coward I am.”

Everything becomes clear... It's often said that confusion prevents action. I've been in a state of confusion for the past 20 years. Of course, there have been many actions, but not in the right direction. My therapist was partly right; I would change my life every two years to solve my problems but, as long as they remained unconscious, I was putting my energy in the wrong place. It seems like I never truly planned out my life. When I was between 16 to 18 years old, I attempted to give it some direction, but things didn't go as expected. Now, as I reflect and write these lines, I can't help but wonder if the universe again conspired. Just as Poli mentions in her chapter, everything happens for a reason.

So I was navigating blindly, trying to escape something, running around like a headless chicken. Traleg Kyabgon, in The Essence of Buddhism, says, “A mind that is stable but without clarity is deficient.” During the past 20 years, I tried to stabilize my mind, but I never gave it clarity, and that's why it was deficient. That's exactly what made me so depressed.

So, it was time to react. I owe it to this unborn baby, to these two incredible children who are already here in my home and, besides, I have no choice. If I continue like this, I'm heading towards disaster. I've always believed that anything is possible, it is just a matter of energy and perseverance, and that's how I built my life. Well, without direction, it's true, but with a lot of energy and perseverance. It's now time to recalibrate, to align with my true path, to reimagine my universe, realign my values, and forge the compass that shall guide me. How can I encourage my children to fight for their happiness in the future if I don't do my best for mine now? A wind of freedom blows across my face. 10 years later, in my coaching sessions, I often say, "Clarity is key," and we work on that. We focus on creating a vision, a direction, a purpose. We redesign our ideal lives to truly understand our deep aspirations. Brian Tracy says: "The greater clarity you have about your mission - the reason why you are on this earth - the easier it will be for you to hit your bull's-eye in life and to measure your success." I couldn't agree more. For me, success is fulfillment.

I learned my first lesson: "Clarity is key." And I made a promise to myself: "Never ever use people and circumstances to run away from your problems." Plan, take responsibility, and be the CEO of your life. It's December 2013, Adrian and Martin's birthday, but we could also say that it's my rebirth, my first anniversary of my new life.

Maybe you feel relieved reading these lines, or maybe you feel discomfort. You're probably thinking, "Phew, she didn't ask the question that would require introspection", the one that would make you quickly review your life to see if, like me, you use circumstances and people to avoid your problems. I won't ask you that question. It's up to you to decide if you want to open that door to clarity. But if you choose to do so, be gentle with yourself and celebrate your courage.

With my trained eye now, I can say that at some point we all have this blind spot, this confusion that leads us to find temporary Band-Aids. And that's all well and good, but these temporary Band-Aids are no substitute for in-depth intervention and healing. So be cautious and take good care of yourself and your wounds.

The change

The first decision I made was to be content with what is.

"Okay, we won't have a third child, and I'm not happy with my job, but I have two healthy boys, a husband who excels in many aspects and is a good father, so life is good."

"We have enough money, I have some financial resources and we live in a country with technology that makes things easy, so life is good."

"I am educated, I can speak several languages, everything is possible, so life is good."

I always rolled my eyes at those 'gratitude, peace, and love' exercises. They seemed to have a talent for cranking up my irritation. But, wait for it, this time was a game-changer: I actually got it!

As a result, a wave of gratitude has settled into my life.

The second decision was to stop moping around and start thinking of solutions.

What can I do to redesign my life the way I want?

What can I do to stop reacting, and being a puppet to the world, and start acting, planning?

My time was very limited as a mom of 2 small children, and working full time and traveling, so I needed to act smartly. I enrolled in a distance coaching certification (back in 2013, it wasn't online, I received my assessments via post, crazy how the world changed). Psychology has always fascinated me. Four years prior, I already wanted to study psychology, but coaching is definitely closer to my heart.

As a result, a feeling of hope overwhelmed me.

The third decision was to stay focused on my goals, despite adversity. My husband wasn't thrilled with my choices. I learned to stand firm, to say "yes" to what aligned with my vision and "no" to what no longer did.

I learned to simplify my life to gain time and energy.

I learned to identify what energized me and decrease activities that drained me.

I learned to organize my schedule and optimize my time as much as possible.

One of a mother's fears is being too involved at work and neglecting her children's fundamental needs. Well, I am no different, it was my fear too. So, I put processes in place to make sure I was there for them and to always be aware of what they needed.

My ideal life and vision are defined by five main ideas: fun and functioning family, love, fulfilling work, health, impact. Take a minute, if you wish, and think about what yours would be...

As a result, I felt at peace and focused.

Becoming the CEO of my life

It took me 2 years and 10 hours of study time per week. I obtained my first certification with the highest possible grade.

We had a big surprise in January 2014. Baby number 3 was going to join our family in September. Like a miracle, like a mystery, or ... is it the universe again? This baby decided to come exactly at the moment when I had fully embraced that I would never have a third child, as if it had decided that now was the right time to enter our family; that now he wasn't coming to save me but to live out his own destiny.

Here's what I have learned from my journey toward a meaningful life, and it has been reinforced with my clients. This quest for more meaning may seem superficial at first, and yet it touches the deepest part of our soul. It's about the meaning of our lives, about the treasure that is life and the proper use of this precious time. It's about what makes us different from animals, this ability to rise in the pyramid of Maslow and reach the need of Self-actualization, the desire to reach our full potential.

Since that day in December 2013, when I understood the

importance of consciously designing my life, of pursuing my ultimate purpose, I never experienced depression again. NEVER EVER. That truly amazes me. Maybe it is not known enough but published literature on life purpose suggests that people with increased life purpose have less depression and anxiety, improved self-acceptance, and more social connectedness, among other important health outcomes.

The journey toward finding my life purpose has been winding, complicated, and challenging. I cried, I felt exhausted, afraid of this new path I was designing, and I continued to feel lonely for a long period of time, but the emptiness was gone, and a new strength replaced it. It would have been somewhat easier to remain employed, in a well-paying job, but I would have only missed out on my life, surviving in a gilded prison in a world lacking in meaning. I would have missed myself, remaining a shadow of myself. And, honestly, I wouldn't have much hope for success in my personal and love life under such circumstances.

Today, I proudly proclaim that I am the CEO of both my life and my business. In 2015, I took a leap and started my coaching business while working part-time as an engineer. I started to teach mindfulness to all ages and help with Leadership/Team building. This decision forced me to change employers because my previous ones didn't support my desire to work part-time. Despite the skepticism from others, who said it was impossible to do my job part-time, I proved them wrong. It was a powerful reminder that with determination, anything is achievable – even finding hidden paths to a new job and to success.

In 2018, I took the natural step of leaving my engineering job as my coaching business flourished. Then, in 2020, I founded the Freedom Catcher Academy, empowering women to create fulfilling and successful careers while balancing other important aspects of their lives.

Impact

In my coaching sessions, I guide teams, people, especially women in their quest for purpose and fulfillment.

Throughout our sessions, I witness incredible transformations. Some choose to alter their careers, embarking on new paths or even starting their own businesses. Others prioritize personal growth by embracing a healthier work-life balance. Relationships within families grow stronger, and some embrace the adventure of moving to new places. As these women make life-altering changes, a remarkable shift occurs within them.

I'd like to share something important. I often hear this phrase: "I can't do that because of my children, I can't work full-time because of my children, I can't start this business because my husband doesn't want me to." Remember, don't let people or circumstances become excuses to avoid pursuing your dreams. Think about that: perhaps you should do it precisely because of them.

Every day, I am inspired by the impact of my choices. My children, who are, at the moment I write this chapter, 13, 12 and 9 years old, look up to me with pride, witnessing their mother's evolution into a more vibrant, present, and supportive figure in their lives. My relationship with my husband flourishes again, where two strong individuals deeply admire and accept one another and my sense of humor has returned. Most importantly, the impact I have on my surroundings expands.

My own children are growing up as remarkable individuals, strong and special. The environment of peace, solidarity, understanding, and trust that my processes and rules have cultivated is yielding remarkable results. This nurturing atmosphere enables them to thrive and find their unique places in the world. Most importantly, they follow their parents' example, working towards organizing their lives for happiness, instilling in them the integrity to pursue their dreams in their own distinctive ways.

They wholeheartedly embrace challenges they are passionate about, and I am now at the right place to discuss and support their aspirations. They exhibit independence, openness, and communicate with gentleness. I firmly believe that none of this would have been possible if I had remained in my old life. The deliberate design of my life has propelled it to another level, both personally and professionally.

Sometimes I hear, "Yes, but your children are different." I believe my children are both ordinary and unique at the same time.

We are all unique in our own way, each with a set of strengths and hidden excellence within us. I once heard a French philosopher say that our environment often teaches us to cultivate our weaknesses and forget about our intelligence, our 'something special'. This made me question where I might still be limiting myself and where I might be limiting my children as well. It is a journey, a lifestyle to evolve toward our potential, happiness, freedom.

With each client who takes this journey with me, gains clarity, uncovers their potential, and transforms their life, a beautiful ripple effect is set in motion. I can see the positive impact they have on their world as they carry their newfound wisdom and strength into their relationships, work, and communities. I can see the ripple effect on their own amazing children, too. Together, through our collective actions and influence, we can shape a world that is more compassionate, equitable, and sustainable. It goes far beyond mere selfish self-actualization; it's a shared actualization. They develop a genuine altruistic behavior, caring deeply about others and striving to create a better world for everyone. This is the ultimate peak of Maslow's pyramid, where the entire world benefits from the radiance of shared actualization.

Find your people

Together, we're creating a better future - one brave woman at a time. This feeling is amazing to me.

When I was 10, heading to school, I promised myself not to talk about my problems anymore. It didn't seem to help, and it felt like nobody really understood.

Now, I'm learning to open up again, trust the right people and solve problems together. Imagine sharing coffee with these wonderful individuals, discussing issues within a caring community driven by a desire to nurture the beautiful, sustainable, and life itself. Can you sense the excitement of this vision? I no longer wonder, “Why am I here?” I know why, and it makes me happy. What's even better is that I'm not alone in this vision.

With this book, you're already part of an amazingly caring community. Each story here is moving and inspiring, reminding us of our incredible inner power. Connect with the authors and tap into the beauty of humanity within yourself and others. This, I believe, is another important key to success that I am still learning.

As these connections develop, our inner wiring shifts, drawing the right people and projects into our lives. Living consciously means making daily choices that align with our inner values - for me, it translates into carefully selecting projects and people while embracing authenticity, honesty, and humility in my interactions and work.

I am writing these last lines from a Blackpool hotel on a windy Monday morning. My son, after completing a 5-day international Street Dance competition, still sleeps. It's been an unforgettable event, with people coming from everywhere on this planet. As I gaze at the sea with a steaming cappuccino nearby, gratitude fills me, reinforcing my ‘wiring Theory’.

I explain myself: My son joined a dance academy one year ago, kind of by accident. Over the past eight months, we've spent a lot of time with the other kids, parents, and trainers, while traveling together for the competitions. This newfound community is amazing. Every interaction leaves me feeling happy, excited, and filled with creative energy. It's a dream community for my son, and I couldn't have imagined anything better.

In the past six months, I've naturally become a part of their journey, as a mental coach, helping with emotions, communication, and thoughts. It all happened effortlessly, like it was meant to be. Is it the power of our inner wiring, or maybe the universe doing its thing? I believe it's both. It is just that 'like attracts like'. When similar things come together without resistance, it allows creative energy to flow. Together, we're creating an awesome dance school and shaping strong, talented kids for a brighter future. It's just an example; I could share more examples of amazing communities I've been fortunate to stumble upon, through chance encounters, connections, or simply having our antennas pointed in the right direction. Once again, I'm learning a valuable lesson: "Find your people, and magic will follow."

It's time to rouse my son and continue our journey to Manchester before heading back home. I'd like to close this chapter with one of my favorite quotes that could summarize it all:

"Find clarity in your purpose, strength in your actions, love in your heart, and you'll make an impact that resonates far beyond measure."

I hope my story resonates with you and stirs something within. If you've decided to open the door to clarity and embrace your freedom, I'd be delighted to connect, listen to your story, and learn about your journey towards a new conscious life. Take care.

CHRISTELLE PILLOT

Christelle Pillot, a seasoned career coach, seamlessly blends success and well-being. Specializing in empowering women, she helps them build rewarding careers while maintaining balance. With a background in Chemical Engineering, her shift to Sales Management revealed a deep interest in human dynamics.

Over 15 dynamic years, she expanded businesses, fostered diversity, and embraced entrepreneurship. Despite external achievements, a profound internal transformation led her to prioritize authenticity.

Since 2013, rooted in meditation, a technique she discovered at 8 years old, Christelle teaches mindfulness, stress management, and emotional intelligence for 3 to 77 years old. Her expertise in business and mental health coaching has made her a guiding force.

As a Business Building Specialist, she mentored during 3 years entrepreneurs, sharing her wisdom nationally and internationally.

In 2021, she founded the Freedom Catcher Academy, uplifting women personally and professionally.

Christelle's approach celebrates uniqueness, optimizes careers, and strengthens connections. Under her guidance, women find happiness, tranquility, and the energy to pursue their dreams. Ready for a harmonious blend of success and well-being?

www.christellepillot.com

5

STRONGER THAN WE KNOW

BY LAUREN J. BUCKNER

As I sit here, outside on my grandmother's porch, the January cold air is stinging my skin, and these freezing wooden steps feel as if they're piercing through my body. I can hear the voices inside the house murmuring. At first, it was hard for me to make out any words because of this fog. My head is just messed up, I can't believe that Mom died. It's been a week already and no one knows what to do with us. Figures, for most of my 15 years on this earth my life has been riddled with uncertainty, abuse, and now abandonment. What are they talking about? They've been in there forever and it's getting colder and colder on these steps. I'm so anxious I really can't wait any longer. I wonder if I can stretch my ear from the steps to the door to hear some of the plans. Probably not. I'll just sit here with my little sister and brother and huddle with them to keep warm. I'm trying to hold it together but I'm super scared and sad. Why is it taking so long? Oh wait, they're getting louder and I think I can make out the words. I can hear a male voice ask, "Did she leave any money behind?" And then another voice, "I can't take them," and then another voice "I can't either." The voices are stopping, it's quiet. The door opens and I gaze up as the adults silently exit the house, walking down the same steps that we're sitting on. Is anyone going to say anything to us? I start to pull my siblings close to me to protect them from the silence because I know what it means.

No one wants us.

The plan would be for us to stay with my grandmother for the meantime. I felt unwanted, unworthy, and abandoned. Alone.

Never again

Growing up, there were so many dark times that it seemed as if life had chosen me as its punching bag. I often felt alone and isolated and struggled to survive. I was raised by a single mother who had untreated mental health issues and who became an alcoholic. I grew up with 3 siblings, an older brother and a younger sister and brother. We all had different fathers, none of which were in the picture. Life was hard for my mother, and she found solace in drinking. The drinking would later evolve into a full-blown alcohol addiction and my mother lost the power to fight. On January 12, 1992, my mother died from cirrhosis of the liver.

For the majority of my childhood, I lived in and out of poverty. We lived in places that weren't fit for living. 'Homes' where there was no water, no heat or electricity. Food was scarce. It was very common for us to run out of food because my mom traded our food stamps for vodka and Benson & Hedges Ultra-Light Menthol cigarettes. How do I know? Because she would send me to the corner store to make the exchange. An envelope for a brown bag. Barely tall enough to reach the counter, I would place the envelope inside the glass window and wait for my package. Very dark times.

But survival was the goal and, so at an early age, I learned how to provide for myself. I would get up in the mornings and walk through the alleys to find aluminum cans to take to the scrap yard. Scrap yards accepted aluminum for a cash payment and I could use that money to eat. I remember climbing in and out of city trash cans, tearing through trash bags with my handmade spear in search of a shiny soda can. By the time I was 10 or 11, I had already created a babysitting business, working for my family and the owner of our local food pantry. I lined up overnight babysitting jobs for the weekends. I didn't really charge much, I didn't care so much about the money, what I wanted most was some stability, a clean, safe place to sleep and a refrigerator full of food. I chose to fight through the hardship and lack...but let me be clear, I hated it!

Poverty...Uncertainty...Lack of Control. I despised that life, and I made a commitment from the core of my existence - 'Never Again.'

Have you ever had a 'Never Again' moment?

Never again would I be hungry, without food or money... Never Again would I be unable to control my life. I was resilient and determined to find a better life. This was my commitment...Never Again.

Being seen

First grade marked the clear change in the direction of my life. The mother that I once knew was about to fade and the security that I felt would be brutally stripped from me, leaving me scared and unprotected. In first grade, our home burned down. We lost absolutely everything. We escaped only with the clothes on our back. My mom owned our house and she had worked hard to purchase it by herself. It was one of her greatest accomplishments to be able to provide a home for our family. As we stood outside the burning house, I watched my mom sob uncontrollably. She didn't speak, but she didn't have to. I could hear her heart breaking, through her silence. My mom would never recover from that loss and my life would never be the same.

The impact of the fire was felt immediately. We didn't have any clothes and so my school conducted a clothing drive for my family. I was so embarrassed, I felt ashamed coming to school wearing my classmates hand me downs. We moved in with my grandmother and depression began to seep into my mother's soul. It would take a few more years for it to become prevalent to me, but I am sure that this is also when her drinking began. We had no home of our own, very little money, and no one to save us. For the next few years, I went to school hungry and unkept. When I got on the school bus I tried to transport myself into what I would describe as a parallel universe of happiness. I would do my best to forget the second-hand, oversized clothes that I often wore and the sadness that resided in my heart and instead imagine myself showing up as anyone other than me.

I didn't want anyone to see ME - but thank goodness someone did!

That someone was one of God's personal angels and she came to me in the form of my first-grade teacher, Mrs. Doris Smith. She saw me. I remember her taking me by the hand one day and guiding me into a room. I didn't know what was happening, but I trusted her. She pulled out a bag of clothes, some with price tags still on them, and she told me they were for me. For me! I was overjoyed. She would always grab my face and tell me how smart I was, and special, and give me the best hugs. Sometimes they were the only hugs I would receive. At home, my presence had begun to agitate my mother and so I did whatever I could to mute myself and be invisible. But Mrs. Smith 'saw' me even when I wanted to shrink and disappear and, without saying much, she cared for me and I let her.

I soon longed to go to school because it was a place where I felt safe and where I learned that I could take care of myself. I grew up in the best era ever, the '80s, where they rewarded kids for being good citizens and reading tons of books. I used to aim to be the best student, because good students got rewards... edible rewards! I must have read a million books (maybe not a million, but a lot) in elementary school so I could earn Pizza Hut BOOK IT points. BOOK IT points could be redeemed for a FREE personal pan pizza. A lightbulb went off in my head and I realized that I could use my brains to feed myself. I worked harder and harder to get As and smiley faces on my assignments, and I was rewarded with a treat from the snack box or an extra item at lunch.

I quickly realized that education was my best path and, most likely, my only way forward to the life that I desired. I latched onto education and all the activities, opportunities and methods of escape from my reality that it could provide; it was my savior. I learned to dream in school and to manifest my ideal life. The signs were all around me, literally. Classrooms were plastered with lamented signs that read, "Nothing is Impossible"... "If You Can See It You Can Achieve It" ... "Dare to Soar." I read those signs every day and I believed every word they said. I would say the words to myself out loud, they served as my personal soundtrack. I began to paint the life that I wanted, one full of happiness, money and endless options.

I pushed through elementary and middle school and all the way through high school with honors. College was next and I was determined to go but college required money and a plan, neither of which had been laid out for me by my mother before she died. This was yet just another obstacle in life that I would need to overcome to get to my next destination. I made an appointment to meet with my high school counselor to discuss my options for college. She helped me review my prospective financial stack, there would be some scholarships for academics and community service but there was an undeniably large funding gap. At that time, I was living with my great-aunt, she had taken me in after living with my grandmother for a few months after my mother's death. She was considered my legal guardian, but had not adopted me. While my great-aunt supported and encouraged my efforts to continue my education, she made it clear that she was unable to provide funds for college. I didn't have anyone to fall back on for financial support. I needed to find a way, and I did. I learned that I could apply for federal financial aid myself if I was deemed an independent student, which meant that I needed to either qualify as an orphan or a ward of the court. I wasn't a ward of the court, but was I an orphan? I mean, yes, I always felt like I was parentless and alone, but what was actually required by law? I got laser focused and found out that both of your parents needed to be deceased to qualify as an orphan. I could clearly prove that my mother was deceased, but not my father. I did not know him, I had never ever in my life seen him. I had been told different stories about his whereabouts, one that included that he died the day I was born, but the truth is I just didn't know anything about him. It would take me several months of making phone calls, filing affidavits, and running down my original birth certificate, to check the 'orphan' box for my college financial aid application. I was awarded federal grants and loans in an amount sufficient to fill my money gap and got accepted to Cornell College! Nothing was going to stop me. I excelled in college and got the opportunity to travel abroad to Guatemala and Bolivia to study and experience different cultures. Me?? The little girl from St. Louis, Missouri who rummaged through garbage bins looking for cans and who ate from food pantries...Me! I was finally winning!

The ability to travel and to live in other countries opened my eyes and marked my liberation from my past. The sensation of my new found freedom swept through every fiber of my being. With each new adventure, it felt as though I was shedding the heavy chains of the past, embracing a future that stretched infinitely before me. I had this profound belief that I could now conquer any obstacle, surmount any challenge, and soar to heights I previously thought unreachable. I wanted to change the world, so I decided that my next best move would be to attend law school. I applied to St. Louis University School of Law and was accepted for admission.

Being a rainbow

I now had what I thought was a clear plan forward. Well, they say if you want to make God laugh, tell him your plans. It turns out God wasn't done humbling me yet. I had walked into a new life and I was done with that old life, but that old life wasn't quite done with me. I still had some Blessings to collect and there was still work to do.

Honestly, I thought that I had taken a beating from life before but my entire foundation was about to be snatched from underneath me and my strength tested. I remember it so clearly, it was the moment my life changed forever and my true purpose in life was revealed...it was the day I surrendered myself to become the rainbow in someone else's cloud.

First year of law school had wrapped and I was in the middle of my summer internship at one of St. Louis' top law firms. I was in my office preparing to shut down for the day when I received a call that my sister was in labor. I gathered my things as quickly as I could and scurried off to the hospital, my sister was bringing another baby into this world. My feelings were super mixed and all over the place. I wasn't sure exactly how I felt about another baby because my sister was already struggling with one child. But I knew I just needed to get there and I needed to get there quickly.

When I arrived at the hospital my sister was already in labor. There were quite a few people in the room, and I noticed from the corner of my eye that there was a Hispanic man sitting next to my sister's bed. Who was he? He wasn't the dad or a family member, so why was he sitting right next to her during labor? There was so much going on and within a blink of an eye a baby came out, a little boy. And just like clockwork, people got up moving like machines. The Hispanic man started to read the words, "We the State of Missouri hereby take custody of baby boy Buckner..." Nurses hurried in and out slapping the baby, shaking the baby and putting IVs in the baby. My brain focused and I noticed that the baby was not really screaming, that he wasn't curled into a ball like most newborns but instead he was sprawled out like a spread eagle and slightly flopping like a fish out of water. I had no idea what was happening at that moment, but I would later learn that this is what it looks like when a drug-exposed baby is born.

My sister was a heroin addict and she had been shooting up when she went into labor. The baby was high.

I immediately began conversations with the hospital social workers and the Hispanic man who turned out to be a Missouri Child Abuse and Neglect (CAN) worker. Lab tests were quickly ordered to determine which drugs were in the baby's system. Tests would later reveal that he was born addicted to heroin and exposed to cocaine. The discussion quickly turned to plans for emergency foster placement and I remember feeling as if my chest was going to explode. I was having a hard time breathing and understanding what was happening. The CAN worker began telling us that my sister would need to go through a drug treatment program and that the baby would be placed in a foster home. Everyone started talking and the voices seemed to get louder and louder, yet I couldn't understand what they were saying. It was as if Charlie Brown's teacher was speaking through a megaphone. The only words that stuck and kept running through my head were "emergency placement", "foster care", "drug exposed". What was happening? I could see the nurses moving the baby from across the room and so I tried to separate myself from the group to get to him, but before I knew it, they whisked him off and out of the room. Where were they taking him? Would he be alone? My heart sank and all I could think was that he was going to be by himself. Alone. Alone like I felt that cold day in January.

The feeling of being alone is as cold as ice, as cold as my grandmother's wooden steps where I sat hoping to be chosen. And now I could feel it all over again, the burning pain from the stinging freezing wood going through my skin, the same pain in my heart...the cold. I tried to physically shake the memory off and pull myself back into the moment, but the feeling, the sensation was so real. It was real and it hurt. Recalling that pain served as the powerful catalyst that snapped me back into the present moment, prompting me to yell out, "I'll take him...he can come home with me." Heads spun quickly and the room fell silent. All eyes were on me and the people in the room gazed at me with a mixture of astonishment and admiration, their faces reflecting a profound sense of wonder and awe, as if they had witnessed something truly extraordinary. I repeated my declaration, "I'll take him, he can come home with me." There would be no more loneliness on my watch, no one else would be left behind.

So many things were happening so fast. I remember talking with my sister and telling her that I would care for the baby while she went through treatment. My baby sister. The baby sister that I named, the baby sister that I cared for many days and that I loved so much that I would give my life to make sure that she was ok. I was scared for her and I was scared for her baby, but I was determined to do everything I could to save them both. She and I chatted about a name and I suggested that she name him Joshua Matthew and she agreed.

I didn't stay by my sister's side long because I wanted to find out where they had taken Joshua. I discovered that he was in the "Special Care Nursery" where he would be closely supervised and made as comfortable as possible to reduce the risks of drug complications. He would also be evaluated to determine the appropriate medications to decrease his withdrawal symptoms. Baby Joshua would have to remain in the Special Care Nursery until all of the drugs were out of his system, an estimated 30 days.

After everything slowed down, I made my way to the Special Care Nursery. I just wanted to hold Joshua and tell him that everything was going to be alright. But, to my surprise, I was denied access. I couldn't visit with him because I was not yet on his approved visitation list. He was now a ward of the State of Missouri and there were rules and caseworkers and a lot of roadblocks between me holding baby Joshua. I could see through the glass, and he was crying and hurting...he was by himself in a room full of other drug babies; babies all fighting to kick an addiction and for a chance at life. I couldn't leave him alone, I just couldn't, so I stood at the nursery window for hours looking at him and talking to him through the glass. I did this for two days while I waited for my visitation approval. I know he couldn't hear me, and I'm not sure if he sensed my presence, but I was there.

It would take almost 48 hours for me to get approved to properly visit with the baby. It felt like an eternity. The Special Care Nursery is one of the saddest places I have ever experienced. The first day as I walk in, I'm greeted by babies screaming, not crying, but screaming. Screaming because they're going through withdrawal. They are in pain. Baby Joshua is not exempt, he's also screaming from the pain. I quickly make my way to Joshua. The moment I cradle him in my arms for the first time, I'm completely enveloped by a profound sense of warmth and an overwhelming feeling of pure, tangible love. He has flawless, velvety chocolate skin, and a perfect button nose with delicate lips. I just can't help myself, I have to press my nose against his and when I do, he smiles and I discover that my precious Joshua has two huge, gorgeous dimples. This baby is an exquisite beauty. As I gently kiss his forehead, he opens his eyes, his long eyelashes batting at me as if to say "hi" and I know, in this moment, that I have made the right decision.

Hug therapy

Baby Joshua had a long, hard journey ahead of him. He had to kick heroin. I didn't know anything about heroin or its effects, but quickly learned from the nurses that heroin is an opioid and causes a physical addiction. Joshua and many of the other babies were experiencing muscle spasms, convulsions and body pain. Opioid withdrawal in a newborn causes central nervous system excitability, such as tremors, stiff or rigid muscle tone and gastrointestinal issues like vomiting and loose stools. The onset of withdrawal symptoms can start anywhere from within the first 48-72 hours after birth. Withdrawal for Joshua would be an extremely painful process.

The doctor initially treated the baby with methadone to treat his heroin dependency. Methadone helps to decrease withdrawal symptoms and relieves drug cravings. Unfortunately, methadone is also an opioid and is addictive. The idea is to give the baby just enough methadone to reduce their symptoms, and then slowly, over days or weeks, decrease that dose to zero. Another treatment method to combat withdrawal pain and spasms is swaddling and I could see from Joshua's chart that his doctor had highly recommended daily hug therapy for him. Daily hug therapy? What did that mean and who was to provide daily hugs? I needed more information.

"Excuse me ma'am, can you explain this note on Joshua's chart? What is hug therapy?" I asked the nurse on duty.

"Interactions like rocking and holding drug addicted babies soothes them and will help reduce the length of your baby's stay in the hospital, " she replied.

I still didn't understand what hug therapy was so I asked again. "But what exactly is hug therapy?"

"Oh, hug therapy is just you holding and hugging your baby tight and close to your body" she explained, she went on to share that drug babies aren't able to soothe themselves.

"Hugging the baby consistently each day for long periods of time will calm him while he goes through the painful effects of drug withdrawal," the nurse explained.

"Long periods of time?" I questioned out loud. "Yes," she responded, "if you can hug him for at least 1-2 hours a day that would be really helpful. Plus, it will help you both bond and create a trusting relationship." I was trying to process this information and I must have looked confused because she gently touched my arm and said, "don't worry if you can't be here, we try to hold each baby at least once a day."

I was taken back by her statement because the room was full to capacity with screaming drug babies and there were only 2 or 3 nurses on duty. In my mind, there was no way that they would have time to hold each baby, especially little Joshua.

I was in the middle of my first summer internship at a large law firm with a full work schedule. My days began at 8am and ended around 5pm, with the obligatory summer associate evening networking events. I couldn't be in both places at one time. My head started spinning and I think I blacked out for a moment, but I was jolted back into reality by the screaming cries of the babies. The screams of pain. The screams from babies who had no one there to comfort them. I knew what I had to do...whatever it took. The next day, I told my mentor at work about the situation and expressed that this was an emergency. I didn't go all the way into detail about the drugs because, honestly, I was embarrassed to tell this well-off white woman that I needed to care for my drug-addicted nephew. I simply told her that the baby was sick and that I needed to support my sister. Technically, I didn't lie. To my surprise the firm was understanding and allowed me to alter my work schedule to care for Joshua. And so, for almost 30 days straight, I came to the hospital to hug and hold my little Blessing for hours and hours. I would come to the nursery before and after work and in between my foster parenting certification classes. I made it my priority to be there to hold him on my belly, to sing to him and kiss him and to just help him as he fought. His small body would tremble from the withdrawal pain, and I would pull him closer and hold him tight against my chest in hopes that I might be able to absorb some of his discomfort. Back and forth we would rock until he found peace; and after he was settled we would just gaze into each other's eyes. He was the strongest person I knew.

Next best move

The decision to foster Joshua was a decision that I made instantly. I did not consult with anyone. I made it with the best interests of both my sister and Joshua in mind, I wanted them both to have a chance. My sister was sad and scared, and I don't blame her. She was being sent off to rehab and told that her drug-addicted baby would be placed in a foster home. Josh's dad was in jail when he was born, so he didn't offer any support. My sister's world was blowing up and I wanted so badly to protect her. For the first part of her life, I was her keeper, I cared for her as if she was my own. She was 9 when my mother died and we were separated. She stayed with my grandmother, and I went to live with my great-aunt. Our lives went into different directions and I was no longer able to care for her or protect her. It was heartbreaking. I never imagined in a million years that we would be at this point, my sister battling a drug addiction and the possibility of losing her child to the system. My baby sister had fallen, and I wanted to be there to catch her. Baby Joshua was an extension of my sister and so he was also an extension of me. I had always strived to be 'my sister's keeper' and if ever there was a time to protect her it was now.

I sat down to chat with my great-aunt after my decision just to bring her up to date. During our discussion she cautioned me, "don't do it Lauren, it will ruin your life." "This is not your fight; you have your own life to live," she urged me. She had a point. I was 26 years old, single, and finally living life on my own terms. I felt like the world was my oyster. I had plans to return to Bolivia after law school and to serve as an international playmaker. I was going to live out all the dreams I dreamt gazing at my elementary school posters.

"What will happen when or if his parents come back?" my great-aunt asked.

"I don't know," I replied, "I really have no idea."

The questions and the inference that I do nothing and just leave Joshua blew me away. I expected more support from her, she herself had taken me in when I had no one. This was my blood, my sister's child. She saw a risk and a liability, but I saw my nephew. He was my family and, at this point, I was all he had. Do you think that I could just abandon him? He was a real live person. He didn't ask to be part of this horrible cycle. I just thought to myself: "Now is the time to break the generational curse Lauren and to show up for your family." No one else was going to step up. If it was meant to be, it would be up to me. So I brushed off all skepticism and prepared for my next best move...motherhood.

Fear of the unknown

As the weeks went on, my sister's progress stalled. I found out that she stopped her drug treatment and checked herself out of the rehab center. I had spoken to her a few times while she was there, and I knew that she was struggling. She didn't want to stay. She was hurting, in pain, and mentally she wasn't ready.

I knew first-hand that beating the heroin addiction wasn't easy because of my experience with Josh. I remained hopeful and continued to encourage her when we spoke. When I learned that she had left rehab, I was disappointed but not surprised.

Unfortunately for my sister, the family court system didn't have the same forgiving heart that I had. A status hearing was called to provide the court with an update on any progress and to determine the next steps. Back to court. So, now I'm sitting here in court, waiting for the judge to finish reading the case notes and I'm really feeling sick. My stomach is in knots because of the stress and anxiety of the unknown.

"Thank you for your patience," the judge said. "This court initially ordered emergency short-term placement for the infant; however, due to the mother's noncompliance the placement plan must be modified. I am recommending that the infant's placement be upgraded to short-term placement to include anywhere from an additional three months up to two years."

"Ms. Buckner, are you still willing and able to provide care for the infant?" he asked me.

"Yes, your honor I am."

"So ordered, court is adjourned," the Judge declared as he pounded his gavel.

And just like that the landscape of our situation changed. My relationship with my sister immediately took a sharp turn and it started to feel contentious. In my mind, we were a team, but she now started to see me as her enemy. Some of my family members started whispering and rumors began to surface that I was attempting to 'take' my sister's baby. People really started to look at me as if I were the villain and that, somehow, I was victimizing my sister. It was awful and it hurt. But I didn't have much time to focus on my family's nonsense because I had real life issues to deal with – I had to prepare for Fall semester with a newborn. Yes, don't forget, I was still in law school. It was mid-August now and classes were set to start in less than 2 weeks. I had real life issues going on and not one of the people on the rumor mill were offering to help me. I needed to focus, and I had to be successful.

Soul pact

Up to this point, Joshua and I were inseparable. How was I going to leave him to attend classes? We had been together almost every day since he was born. No one knew how to take care of my Joshua like me. I couldn't even bear to think about leaving him with anyone, but I had to go to my classes. Everything was hard for me now, every decision that I had to make was hard and frightening. I didn't have a good plan, the only thing I knew to do was to PUSH. So, I did what any irrational new mother would do, I decided to take my 1 ½ month baby to class with me! Yes, I was insane. Completely out of my mind! Now I know that this is going to sound crazy to you (yes crazier than my decision to take Joshua to law school classes), but I made a soul pact with this baby. I picked him up, looked him in the eyes and said, "look I have to go to school and you have to come with me and I need you to be quiet." We had a meeting of the eyes, and an agreement was made. I took Joshua to classes with me every day for almost 3 months. I would place my Boppy pillow on my lap, lay him across it with his pacifier and scoot him under the desk. I periodically looked down to check on him and would catch him quietly gazing up at me. He never said a word. We were a team.

I got into a groove and things got better for me at school and home. Josh required a substantial number of special services and I worked hard to make sure that he got what he needed. Between classes we had pediatrician appointments to check his blood levels and developmental progress. Joshua had a private occupational therapist who came to our home twice a week to assist with his motor skills. He also had a private nurse that came to our home to teach me how to implement everything from his treatment plans. It was a lot to care for Josh, but we were building a system and I felt very encouraged.

Another Blessing

Although Josh and I were creating a rhythm, my sister was not making any progress. At this point I did not have regular contact with her, but I knew that she was back on drugs and engaging in some reckless behavior. I had weekly calls with our caseworker, Ashley, and she provided me with updates. On one call in particular, she informed me that there were concerns for the safety and welfare of my sister's other child, Lee. Lee was three years old, and he lived with my sister and grandmother. Ashley gave me the heads up that they were discussing the possibility of removing Lee from my sister's custody. He would be placed in a foster home if removed. As you can probably imagine, my mind went to town 'planning'. I knew for a fact that no one in our family was going to step up to foster Lee if the State took custody. I already knew that it was going to be me. I was the only option to prevent him from being placed with a traditional foster parent.

What in the world am I thinking?! Right? I'm single and a full-time law student. I'm hanging on by a thread caring for one child - what would it be like with two small children? I also have no job and my savings account is leaning towards empty. The deck is stacked against me. But remember my commitment: Never Again? That commitment was not just for me, it also extended to my bloodline. Never Again would anyone that came after me experience abandonment, poverty or instability.

Never Again. I don't have a plan, but I know that if Ashley calls me and says Lee needs a home that I'm going to say yes. I'm terrified just trying to imagine how this would even work. Me with no plan, just my commitment...but that would have to be enough.

It was mid-October when I got the call that they were taking custody of Lee. He would come to live with me and Josh. He would be with his brother.

Don't quit

We were now a family of three and my faith would be tested. My days usually started in the darkness, as I reluctantly peeled myself from my bed. I tried to get in an hour of outlining case law every morning before the apartment sprung alive with the sounds of children. Our mornings were like Olympic sprints, me flying through the air preparing bottles and making breakfast, trying to feed a toddler and myself, all while getting the three of us dressed and out the door. One of the most significant challenges of my days was the daycare drop off and pickup, my timing had to be perfect. I had to coordinate transportation times with class times and study groups which usually meant a speeding marathon through St. Louis City. After classes, I juggled feeding the boys, changing diapers, taming tantrums and enjoying family time. Family time was priceless. Family, this was what it was all about anyway. And although law school demanded my full attention, and I needed to study, the boys needed me more and they were my priority. So, I made time to love them every day. And somewhere between the children napping and late nights, I seized the opportunity to study.

My multitasking of my responsibilities was relentless, and it was killing me. At some point, I started operating on autopilot and relied on my faith to guide me. I had an unwavering determination and belief that with one more step and then another step I would eventually get us closer to structure, foundation, stability and happiness. If I just kept pushing, I was certain that I could break the generational curses that had been placed upon us. There had to be an escape. There had to be a better way for children to live and exist, a way with no pain. But, it was almost as if the blind were leading the blind. I didn't know how to be a mother. I didn't have a healthy mother model to mimic. Instead, I had to try to mother and love not from a place of familiarity, but from a place of lack. I tapped into all the holes that I had, and all the emptiness that I had experienced my entire life, and used that as my frame of reference as a mother. I parented the boys from the gap, from the places and spaces that existed within me. I was able to outline my blueprint of motherhood by tapping into my pain, my deepest insecurities and fears.

Life started to get really hard for me. It turns out that having a plan probably would've been better than just having my commitment, because my commitment brought me to a moment of humility. I fell flat down on my face and back to a place I vowed never to return.

Look at me, sitting outside the food stamp office, crying hysterically in my car. Unbelievable! Just 6 months ago, I was a 26-year-old, single woman finishing my first year of law school - on top of the world. Now, I've come to the realization that I am out of money. Broke and broken. I don't have enough money to care for the children, MY children. I have to get back on state assistance just to feed us. I'm right back at the front door of poverty, the place I vowed never to return. Me? I failed! I failed and I am pissed, sad, embarrassed and ashamed. How had I gone from poverty and pain to purpose and passion, and right back to poverty and pain? The tears just keep coming, blurring my vision as they land onto my thighs.

I bowed my head in sorrow and defeat. I sat in my car and

waited for some answers, but none came. What did come to me were words from a poem that I had memorized from my mother's obituary, titled Don't Quit. I had often recited the poem to myself as motivation to keep going. It was no surprise that the words found me on this particular day.

"When the funds are low and the debts are high, And you want to smile, but you have to sigh, When care is pressing you down a bit, Rest if you must, but don't you quit...And you never can tell how close you are. It may be near when it seems so far. So stick to the fight when you're hardest hit. It's when things seem worse that you must not quit."

Excerpt from "Don't Quit" by Edgar A. Guest

I let the words of the poem flow through my thoughts and penetrate my mind and I allowed myself to remember who I am. I am a WINNER! Adversity isn't new to me. Hard times are what I am made from. And in between the onset of the sadness of my perceived failure, a profound transformation unfolded within my soul. I felt the dormant energy of resilience ignite within me. I lifted my head and wiped my eyes. I uncovered my reservoir of courage. And despite the uncertainty that lay ahead of me, I decided to hold my head up. I was not built to break.

After my mini nervous breakdown, I had tunnel vision. I was locked in and focused on the target: Survival. I quickly tucked my fear and pain away, there wasn't time to feel. I've found that feelings become distractions. I did use the initial feelings as power to move forward, but then I had to turn the emotions off because they became too raw. I tapped back into my childhood coping strategy of compartmentalizing my feelings and separated those parts of me that were hurting and scared.

Months went by with no positive updates on our case. My sister was still actively using drugs and the boys' father was still incarcerated. By Spring, it was clear to me that our short-term placement was not going to be all that short. It would be me and the boys...and law school.

Loving sacrifice

Over the next two years, I embarked on a relentless journey that demanded every ounce of my strength and resilience. It felt like I was navigating a never-ending storm, trying to steer two ships in opposite directions. The sheer weight of my responsibility as a mom and student bore down on me every single day. The struggle was undeniably hard. Law school was unforgiving, demanding hours of reading, research and writing. I had countless late nights poring over case law while my children slept soundly. The rigorous demands of my studies often left me sleep-deprived and mentally exhausted. The balancing act was arduous, but it was a sacrifice I was willing to make. Education had been my savior before and I was betting on it now to provide a brighter future for the boys.

Sacrifices became an integral part of my life. My first year of law school was carefree, I had plenty of time to study and enjoy time with friends. Now while my friends attended social events and study groups, I often found myself rushing to pick the kids up from daycare, sacrificing much needed breaks and study time. My law school friends did their best to support me with the boys. They shared notes for classes that I had to miss and tried to accommodate my study schedule when possible. The administration allowed me to bring the boys to campus. I often had to pack them up at night to return to school to study, bringing along their blankets and pillows for sleeping pallets. The financial burden was immense as well, as tuition, textbooks, and childcare costs strained my limited resources. But, through it all, I remained resolute in my commitment to excel academically and provide a nurturing environment for my young Blessings.

The most profound sacrifice, however, was my strained relationship with my sister. She struggled with her own battles and was unable to complete her drug court plan, it was crystal clear that I had to prioritize the children. I was all they had. It was an agonizing choice, fraught with resentment and tension. Our relationship deteriorated, as she resented my efforts, and I grappled with the emotional toll of both her absence and my new responsibilities.

My sister thinks I hate her and that I don't love her. Thinking about it just takes my breath away. I wish that she could see that it's the exact opposite. I love her more than I love myself and all I want is for her to know that.

I pressed on despite the heartbreak I felt from my sister, determined to provide a stable and loving home for her children. At this point, everything I did was genuinely for them. I no longer thought about what was best for me or what I wanted. I didn't matter. What mattered most to me was that neither boy was left behind and that they were together.

My last two years of law school tested my resolve. I was pushed to the limits of my endurance. However, amid the chaos and exhaustion, there were moments of pure joy and fulfillment. I witnessed the boys flourish, their smiles and laughter serving as my guiding light. Their resilience and growth in the face of adversity was awe-inspiring, reminding me why I embarked on this challenging path in the first place. Yes, the path was grueling and filled with heartache. That's a fact. But my determination allowed me to not only succeed in law school but to also secure a six-figure offer to join a law firm after graduation. This would cement my ability to offer a lifeline to the boys. With the Finish line clear in sight, I took a deep breath and pushed one more time.

Proudest moment

Graduates please stand. Ladies and gentlemen, I present to you the members of the 2006 graduating class of St. Louis University School of Law.

There are no sweeter words.

On May 20, 2006, with 2 children hip to hip I walked across the stage and was hooded and presented with my Juris Doctor of Law and a certificate in International and Comparative Law. It was the proudest moment of my life, born from the hardest fight I'd ever fought!!! My back was against the wall many times but I chose to push forward. In order to succeed, I had to expand the vision I had for myself and my life. I had to dig deeper than I ever imagined possible, and it turns out that I was much more capable than I thought!

There's so much possibility on the other side of adversity, yet many will never achieve it because they become paralyzed by their circumstances or the limitations placed upon them. Don't let that be you. If you have lived a misplaced life or experienced what seems like the end of the road, I encourage you to believe that you have the ability to create something else.

Anything is possible.

And not all routes are direct. Life has thrown me so many twists and turns, placing me in unfathomable positions that I should have quit. But I didn't. I am free and on the other side of adversity. Today after building a successful 17 year legal career, I have walked away to build my own business and dreams. It's my time. And as I am writing this chapter, Josh has just gone off to start his first year of college and to make his mark in life. I couldn't be prouder.

Through it all, each up and down, I can now proclaim that which I've always believed to be true, which is that you and I, we, are unequivocally stronger than we know.

LAUREN J. BUCKNER

Lauren is an attorney-turned entrepreneur who works with women to help them build a financially, empowered life. Lauren is originally from St Louis, MO and attended Cornell College in Mt.Vernon, IA where she received her Bachelor of Arts degree in Psychology and Spanish. After college, Lauren moved to Bolivia, South America where she worked as an English professor and performed as a professional jazz dancer throughout the region. Lauren returned from Bolivia to attend law school at St. Louis University School of Law where she received her Juris Doctor with an emphasis in International and Comparative Law. Lauren is a seasoned business and real estate development attorney, with a specialization in affordable housing and mixed-use developments. She is the owner of Buckner Consulting, a business consulting firm, where she represents small and mid-sized companies in their general business, contract negotiation and land matters.

Lauren is also known as the Business Builder and helps women build strong businesses on solid foundations to leverage their income and create money babies.

www.bucknerconsult.com

6

THE HEALING ALCHEMY OF FORGIVENESS: TRANSMUTING PAIN AND TRAUMA INTO PERSONAL FREEDOM

BY CARMEN BENTON

In the depths of every human soul, lies a labyrinth of scars and wounds. Some are visible, engraved onto our bodies as a testament to the adversities we have faced. Others are more elusive and reside within the hidden innermost parts of our hearts, unseen but felt deeply. That's what we call trauma and we are all carrying some sort of this type of wound, no matter how seemingly insignificant or profound it might seem. It is within the understanding that we all have some degree of healing to do that I invite you to entertain this chapter and explore the healing alchemy of forgiveness, to transmute your story of pain and trauma into a story of personal freedom.

I am writing this chapter while finally cherishing priceless moments with my daughter, moments for which I have to pinch myself to ensure they are not just a dream, because we are creating bonds I never thought were possible for me to create with her, or anyone for that matter. Over the course of three weeks, we have exciting plans ahead, including visits to Disneyland, attendance at a social media conference where she is hoping to meet her idol and, most anticipated of all, the Taylor Swift Eras tour.

In preparing for these events, I find myself adapting my fashion style to adhere to certain dress codes that my daughter tells me are key to fit in; of course I'm speaking of my sequined outfit and multiple bracelets I'm going to be wearing on the day of the concert.

Over the past six months, I have wholeheartedly immersed myself in the task of memorizing 44 Taylor Swift songs. The upcoming concert has become the centerpiece of our lives, and I've embraced the challenge of not only knowing a few songs, but to embrace the overachiever in me and strive to know every single song by heart.

My technique to memorize these songs have ranged from creating videos for my social outlets featuring them, to sharing stories on social media using the songs in the background, and believe it or not I have even sought to extract meaningful lessons from the lyrics for my transformational posts.

As you can tell my daughter and I are having the best summer, and today I can say that we have a solid and loving relationship. However, this wasn't always the case. The truth is that my journey of joyful experiences with my daughter, Sofia, who is 14 at the time I'm writing this chapter, has only started in the past twelve months, despite the promise I made to myself in my younger years. A promise to be the kind of mother I had longed for. I truly yearned to embody the qualities I desired my mom to show me, but never did. Qualities such as being a loving, caring, funny mom.

My mother, though intelligent and hardworking, taught me responsibility and instilled in me an unshakeable drive for success. She modeled for me how to be a hard worker and never give up and she ingrained in me the belief that if you are going to do something, you better be the best at it. This is exactly what got me to the corner office in corporate America. Yet, the warmth, affection and the simple joys of shared laughter were absent from our relationship. I honestly struggle to recall even a single moment of genuine enjoyment between us, ever.

Growing up feeling abandoned, pushed aside and feeling unimportant to my own mother made me determined to chart a different path for my family, but regrettably, I fell short of my aspirations. This was my self reflection as I realized I had become exactly the person and the mom I never wanted to become.

I possessed intelligence, I was driven and resilient, had achieved so many educational and professional goals, yet I failed to be the mom I always wanted to be. I failed to be present and to show love and affection for my children, especially to my daughter who desperately needed my love and affection just the way I desperately needed both of those when I was a little girl. It was as if I was subconsciously pushing her away, the same way I felt pushed away by my mom. Reflecting back, I think this was because, in a way, she reminded me of myself at that age and all the things I wanted and needed from my mother - but never got. Unfortunately, this is the way trauma survivors of any kind relive their traumas over and over again. It becomes a vicious cycle where your everyday decisions forge the path to ensure you are stuck in the past, forever or until you heal.

The crazy part of all this is that I always wanted her. I even named her before I got pregnant, maybe because I knew we had to go through this journey together?

Throughout the pregnancy, I was so excited that she was coming. I knew I was pregnant with a girl from the moment she was conceived. I remember getting lots of 'girly' baby things and even remodeling the house to make sure she had a nice nursery. I had dreams of my daughter and I being best friends.

I already had my son, Stefan, who was just a toddler and with whom I had a great bond and so I expected it was going to be just like that. But it wasn't. At first, I attributed it to postpartum depression, which I did have, but things didn't change when eventually I got better. I consciously wanted to have this great and amazing bond with my baby girl, but it just wasn't the way I had envisioned it.

I should have gotten the message when the universe decided my daughter's birthday would be the day after mine. Why? Because my birthday is the day after my mom's. So, even when I was not aware that I was acting out the same generational story that my grandma and my mom and I had experienced as children, and repeated as moms, there was a clear sign from the universe from the very beginning that I thought it was pure coincidence. But, I see differently now.

Throughout my childhood, I endured much emotional neglect and abandonment. My earliest memories go from me screaming at the top of my lungs, at the age of two, begging not to be left at the house with my caregiver, to writing behind the bed, at the age of four, as many times as I could fit in behind the headboard: Nobody loves me, nobody loves me, nobody loves me.

This little girl didn't want much, I didn't even care that we were poor. I just wanted my mom to play with me once in a while. I wanted her to cuddle with me, tuck me into bed and show me that she loved me. But, instead, I felt like I was pushed away every time I tried to get close. It was almost as she was rejecting me, because subconsciously she was. She also had a programmed belief in the deepest corner of her heart that the mother-daughter relationship wasn't safe. As I know now, she was also emotionally neglected and abandoned by my grandmother.

Unfortunately, things just got worse after my parents divorced. My mom started dating a new person and he was competing for her affection against me: a stepfather. A creepy stepfather, to be precise. There was something about the way he looked at me and his energy felt scary. His presence was very unsettling and made me feel unsafe, especially when someone decided it was a great idea for him to be allowed to pinch my butt and tickle me - even though I would be screaming for him to stop. This trauma is still so ingrained in me that whenever I hear a girl being tickled and asking the person tickling it to stop, I just want to punch that person in the face.

Why? Because my feelings, fears, and pain were consistently dismissed by my mother. On several occasions, I tried to tell my mom that I felt unsafe around him, that I thought he was always looking at me in a weird way. I also tried to tell her how mean he was to my little brother, who is autistic, and that he kept calling him names. I guess this is why they say that 'love is blind', because she couldn't see it.

"You are making things up." Mom would assert dismissively.

Or...

"Don't be so sensitive, you are just like your father: always exaggerating everything."

Or, my personal favorite, considering my multiple clair abilities...

"You are simply imagining things."

This inevitably left me wondering if she actually loved me. Not only did I not get her affection, I didn't get her protection either.

As time passed, I convinced myself that nobody loved me. I mean even wild animals protect their babies with all their fury, but there I was left to what it felt like being thrown in a cage with a predator; just waiting for me to blink, to attack.

Was it possible I was so desensitized from my pain that, even though the thoughts and memories of my childhood are painful still, I was subconsciously replicating the past? Was it possible that even though I never seek to undermine my role as a devoted mother, the deeply ingrained programming within my DNA, nervous system, and subconscious, aimed to keep me safe?

Of course, yes. The reason being, it is obvious now that in the deepest and most sacred corners of my being, the mother-daughter relationship was not labeled as safe, as it represents painful and unhappy memories for me.

I remember, at the age of 9, that my mom forgot my birthday. I was in the 4th grade and I woke up to nobody remembering it was my special day. My parents were divorced by that time, and my dad worked evenings so I wouldn't hear from him until after school. This was a very sad day for me, as it wasn't until my dad called me in the afternoon to say 'happy birthday' that someone celebrated me then. I literally healed this wound on my 47th birthday when it eventually dawned on me why I had such strict rules about my birthday, and my expectations about how others should celebrate me. On my 9th birthday, I decided that if people didn't acknowledge and celebrate my birthday, they most likely would not love me. I created this rule because the time my mom forgot my birthday caused me much pain and fights on my birthday throughout the years.

Have you experienced any event that might have seemed insignificant but, in truth, left you with scars that play a part in dictating how you behave today?

Despite all this, I grew up admiring my mother and never really realizing that I had any trauma to heal. Looking back, I think it was because when I was growing up we never had any extra money, just enough to pay the rent and buy food. Because of that, I started to convince myself that I should be grateful for the roof over our heads and the food we had to eat. I started to applaud how hard my mom worked, to justify her neglect. I remember thinking that such gratitude should outweigh any longing for safety and happiness I still had on me. After all, if Tina Turner proclaimed that love is just a second hand emotion, who needed a vulnerable heart that could be broken?

Breaking the Chains: Escaping the Cycle of Trauma and Healing the Mother-Daughter Relationship

In 1984, at the age of 9, I internalized the belief that love was a precarious endeavor, not worth entertaining. Instead, I resigned myself to the role of the protector and challenger, solely to survive. It became my duty to shield myself and my brother from the threat posed by my stepfather, becoming hyper alert at a very young age. I found every possible reason for us not to be at home. I joined every after-school activity, every academic club, sport, band activity, etc. Whatever would give me the excuse not to be at home. This is where escapism from my reality as a form of coping mechanism really began.

During the summers, I would escape for the entire three months and flee to my aunt's house. I remember wishing that she was my mom. She was, and is still, so easy to talk to. Always loving, never judging, warm and present. To this day, the bond I developed with my aunt and my cousins, from all those summers at their house, is so strong and special to me. Whenever home, I would spend most of my day in my bedroom, hiding from my stepfather whenever he was around.

You would think that after experiencing the nightmare that was, for me, growing up with an emotionally unavailable mother, in a loveless house, and with that kind of stepfather, I would never do that to my children. Right? Well, here lies yet another way I failed my children - I fell in the same relationship trap that my mom did, not only giving my children a stepfather, but two. I was so familiar with, and yet so oblivious to, this pattern. Until a year ago.

Sofia, my daughter, was always a wonderful child; spirited, witty, smart, funny, and desperate to build a connection with her mother - who was unfortunately emotionally unavailable. I decided to be that kind of a mother, as a coping mechanism, to protect her heart. Even today, it brings tears to my eyes to admit that not too long ago we were strangers living under the same roof. She resented me for my decisions, my choices, my attitude, but above all she resented me for my unhealthy coping mechanisms. I believe that she could not probably verbalize these feelings, they showed in her rebellious behaviors. I witnessed her beginning to close up her heart, just like I had. I started to see how she was numbing herself with school and social media.

As a woman who grew up with a heart closed to emotions, and now faced with the oh-so-many mistakes I've made in life, the only source of the happy hormone I could entertain getting was the dopamine rush I got every time I hit a goal. Besides, working was the most lucrative numbing distraction for my pain that I could come up with.

This pattern started super early in my life, to be precise it started as early as elementary school. I realized that if I did my part I'd get good grades and praise from the teachers. Soon, I started doing more than was expected: getting all the extra credits that I could, participating in every extracurricular activity possible and always going above and beyond. I know now that I was doing all of this mostly to get my mom's praise, not the teachers. But, it became so normal that I would be the best that instead of getting praise when I was the best, I got criticism when I didn't hit the mark. So, I did it more and more and more every time. Still not getting the praise and connection I yearned for from my mom, but too deep in the dopamine cycle to realize that this was a problem.

It was a problem because this is not different from the experience any addict goes through when consuming their drug of choice; there is a common cycle in all addicted behaviors and it is that you always need to up the dose of the drug to feel the same rush as the previous time. This is how people become addicts, and this is how I became a workaholic.

Yes, I became addicted to work and the emotional rewards that came with it.

After having children, and as an adult, workaholism was my socially accepted drug, a drug addiction I couldn't control. Initially, because I wasn't aware of this being a thing , but later because its perceived rewards had so much power and control over me. I used it to numb my pain, escape reality, and avoid both intimacy and vulnerability at all cost. And the more successful I became, the more reasons I had to consume my drug of choice and the less resistance I got from those around me. After all, my addiction was paying for the bills, the travels and the luxuries in our lives.

Unlike a traditional alcohol or drug addict, workaholics usually get encouraged by those around them to keep enduring the behavior. After all, all people could see when they saw me was a shiny steely exterior, like prestige armor, but what they didn't see was that such armor was only concealing my wounded heart. This armor allowed me to achieve remarkable professional success in my life, scaling the corporate ladder with ease, making it to the ranks of top leadership, and becoming a corporate executive in a male-dominated industry. In fact, I was the first Latina to achieve the vice president title in the company from which I retired. Yet, my wounded heart kept my relationships suffering, plagued by my inability to forgive my past traumas and myself.

As I saw my daughter starting to adopt the same numbing and escapist mechanisms I have used throughout my life, I had a face to face moment with myself, full of sadness and regret, where the question: ***What the hell are you doing with your life Carmen?*** came very loud and clear for me. I knew at that moment that I couldn't allow this cycle of pain to continue any further. Should we call this rock bottom?

I knew then that this is where my family's generational nonsense will end. I also knew that to do that, I needed to begin with myself. I needed to heal myself first so that I could heal my relationship with my daughter and my sons too.

In order to do that, I had to start by having compassion for myself. I had to stop being so judgmental about what I do and how I do it. And that was particularly hard because throughout my life I was always judged by my mom about my thoughts, answers and choices, so judgment triggers me hard still.

Hard to believe there was any way out of the pit I carved for myself, but as I write this chapter, I am filled with gratitude for the profound journey I am embarking upon with my daughter now - decades later. This comeback is a testament to the healing and transformation that forgiveness can bring, as I have liberated myself from the chains of the past and created a new narrative of love, joy, and fulfillment... With my daughter.

I have healed the mother-daughter relationship in my lineage.

In case you are telling yourself right now that you are one of the lucky ones that doesn't have to worry about healing trauma, I want to share with you that I have come to recognize that we are all burdened with some form of trauma, regardless of its apparent magnitude. Basically, if you have experienced an emotionally charged event, you have experienced trauma. It could be the weight of childhood abandonment, emotional neglect, sexual abuse, an abusive relationship that chewed at your self-worth, or the subtle scars left behind by years of societal pressure and expectations.

You might actually have experienced more than one traumatic event or traumatic period in your life, like I have. I've shared with you how I decided to close up my heart at the age of 9 as a result of the emotional neglect from my mother. Unfortunately, that didn't shield me from entering narcissistic relationships which created trauma and led me to approach relationships even more scared, resulting in worse relationships and so on.

Also, all the expectations that were placed in me to be successful, to be important, to be independent. Those expectations also created trauma in me, because in a way it was as if I had endorsed my life to fulfill someone else's dreams.

Why am I telling you all of this?

I'm sharing this because I believe that no trauma should be belittled or dismissed, for its impact on our lives can be profound and far-reaching. And it is within this deep understanding that we must cultivate compassion -for ourselves and for others.

Exploring the detrimental effects of pain and trauma on personal well-being

Part of the protector and challenger persona that emerged in me as a coping mechanism, to survive the threats I perceived to have to endure during my childhood and the lack of connection and love I felt growing up, instilled the pressure in me to project the illusion of having a perfect life - one I never truly possessed, not until after healing myself.

Can you see how trauma may shape the way you have been reacting and approaching your life?

In my case, I've come to realize that my traumas have shaped my perspectives, influenced my relationships, and hindered my personal growth. The weight of unresolved pain and trauma can burden you, causing emotional distress, mental anguish, and even physical ailments.

When you carry the weight of pain and trauma within yourself, it acts as a heavy anchor, holding you back from experiencing personal freedom and living life to its fullest. You are basically stuck in the past, day after day, week after week, month after month, year after year.

Unresolved pain can manifest in various ways, such as chronic stress, anxiety, depression, and a general sense of disconnection. It can taint your perceptions, color your interactions, and limit your ability to trust and form deep connections with others.

Carrying my trauma was getting to the point where I couldn't ignore it anymore. It wasn't 'only' emotional anymore. It was fully manifested in my physical reality, as the cumulative stress had taken a toll on my physical health: years of suffering from migraines that culminated in the eruption of nasty, dangerous hives covering my entire body, and painful stomach ulcers that landed me in the hospital.

Also, my need to control everything around me tightened, gradually impacting my interactions with my already emotionally wounded children, and intensifying the toxic patterns of guilt within me. All of this left me feeling utterly dreadful about myself, pushing me towards seeking socially acceptable avenues to numb my pain even further.

However, to truly allow myself to seek the help I needed, I first had to cultivate compassion within myself, to realize asking for help didn't make me weaker, but stronger.

I have witnessed first hand in my own life, the transformative power of compassion and forgiveness and, through this chapter, I want to share it with you. Because, in each scar my soul bears I have found a source of empowerment-a testament to my capacity to rise above adversity. I see this testament in the stories of my fellow warriors featured in this book and also my amazing clients. I find inspiration to continue forging a path toward personal freedom, where wounds no longer define us but serve as markers of our growth and resilience.

Today, I invite you to embark on this journey with me -a journey that celebrates our shared humanity, acknowledges our scars, and embraces the healing alchemy of compassion and forgiveness. With each step, you will reclaim your power, liberating yourselves from the shackles of pain and opening the door to personal freedom. For in the depths of our souls, we are bound by our common journey -a journey toward self-discovery, healing, and a profound connection with the world around us.

Embracing Compassion to Unleash the Power of Forgiveness

At 45 years old, and looking back at my life, I was so ashamed and the only thing that seemed soothing to me was to perhaps continue to numb the pain. But, as if miracles exist, I started to embrace the possibility that maybe there was a reason for all my questionable choices, maybe there was a lesson that once I learned it could lead me to happiness and freedom from the past. When that thought felt slightly hopeful for a second, quickly I could feel my energy shrinking because I was sure that nobody was going to be compassionate towards me. In fact, I was sure that I was going to get nothing but judgment from the world around me. I knew this because as a Catholic girl I knew very well that getting divorced, not once but three times, was going to grant me the keys to hell already. So, if God had already decided I was a bad human, how can anyone else show me some mercy?

I continued to go down the spiral of shame, now also questioning not only my values, but my smarts and it was this moment, right here feeling lonely, shameful, guilty, despicable and unlovable, that I identify as my rock bottom.

I sobbed and sobbed until I had no more tears. My soul was screaming in pain, but it was at this time where I believe I had my awakening experience. The word forgiveness came to mind, and I knew in that instant that I not only needed to forgive myself but that if I wanted to free myself from the pain and trauma, I had to forgive those that hurt me too.

But I had no clue where to start, how to untangle the pain and the thoughts that keep hurting me. How to forget how I had hurt my children the same way I was hurt by my mother? I know now that I was getting guided to my healing, and I was being given the steps to get there, because at the time I didn't know anything about energy and my clair abilities when I clearly heard the word: Compassion.

Compassion is a powerful elixir that allows us to acknowledge the battles fought, the wounds endured, and the strength it takes to persevere. This magical potion helped me move past the mistakes and poor decisions I've made in my life, and weather the storm of an emotionally tumultuous childhood that nearly crushed my spirit beneath the weight of emotional neglect, and the gaslighting I experienced growing up.

I had no clue how to begin to practice self compassion, so I did what anyone would do. I Googled it. The search results included things like: treat yourself as if you love yourself, and also mindfulness. And so, my self love and mindfulness practices started right then.

Embracing the power of mindfulness

Mindfulness is a transformative practice that invites you to fully engage with the present moment, free from judgment or attachment. This is how I began my healing journey.

As it might be for you, mindfulness was extremely hard for me. I couldn't imagine quitting my thinking brain for more than 2 seconds as so many thoughts were always flying by, in all directions. But I kept hearing the benefits of it, so I decided to do one of the things I do best: study. So I started studying meditation, not only the what and the why but the how I could implement such practice into my life.

As I delved into it, I discovered that the purpose of meditation is not to be sitting still thinking about nothing, but to be present in the now. One way to accomplish that is indeed meditation, but there are so many other ways too, including cleaning your house, gardening, painting, cooking, etc.

When I understood the reason behind the method I was

then able to adjust and find other ways that could be used to accomplish the same purpose: to be present.

I discovered that with a little bit of will power I could accomplish a mild sense of relaxation and relief when cooking, cleaning, and even showering, as long as I could keep my mind from going into shame, guilt or blame.

The more I did it, the more I was able to practice mindfulness the traditional way, through yoga and meditation, and with that my ability to observe my thoughts, emotions, and physical sensations without being consumed by them, grew.

Doing things that would keep me in the now became particularly valuable to me when confronting challenging reactions to my emotions and memories linked to pain and trauma, also known as triggers. In other words, when I lost my shit because other people's bullshit triggered my trauma.

So, yes, as time went by and I practiced mindfulness more and more, I used it as a way to consciously interrupt my triggers, which might sound a bit forced and calculated but at the time it was exactly what I needed. Because by cultivating mindfulness, I created a spacious awareness that fostered compassion and non-reactivity, both towards myself and others, and set the stage for forgiveness to flourish.

So did mindfulness heal my traumas? The answer is... Not exactly, but it was the first stepping stone I needed to hit before I was open to receive the tool that indeed helped me heal not only my trauma but my daughter's as well.

Introducing the concept of forgiveness as a healing alchemical process

Once you have embraced compassion for yourself, you have opened the door to the magic of forgiveness and, amidst the shadows of pain and trauma, forgiveness emerges as a transformative force -an alchemical process that has the potential to transmute your suffering into personal freedom.

"Modern alchemy is harnessing the power of forgiveness to transmute pain, transforming trauma into wisdom, strength, and boundless love."

Carmen Benton

The profound truth of this statement resonates deeply with my own personal journey. As I embarked on the path of healing, embracing compassion as my guiding light, I discovered that the initial stride towards transformation was the act of self-forgiveness.

For the longest time, I blamed my pain on others and my life's circumstances: If my parents were not divorced, if my mom was a better mom, if we had more money, if my step dad wasn't a pervert, if my brother wasn't autistic ... life would be better. But then, I was faced with the cold truth, and I mean freezing cold like an ice bath, that I wasn't perfect either and that I had made my own set of regrettable choices along the way, creating the same if not more pain for my children.

Sure, I needed to forgive my step dad and my mom, but I now understood I mostly had to forgive MYSELF for the choices I made fueled by my pain and trauma.

Forgiveness is not about condoning or forgetting the past; rather, it is a conscious and deliberate decision to release the grip of resentment, anger, and bitterness, that keeps you trapped in a cycle of suffering, regardless if it makes sense to your conscious mind or not, because when you are holding resentment in your body it is almost as if you are the starting actor of the Groundhog Day movie. Living your life, waking up to a new day each time, but emotionally experiencing the same shit from the past, over and over.

Harnessing the power of energy healing to welcome forgiveness into my life

I personally didn't seek this path, but I can say today, even with my left brain on, that this path not only found me but saved me and those around me, as energy healing showed me the pathway to opening my heart and embracing forgiveness. Let me share with you how I went from a mechanical engineer, MBA and corporate executive, to an energy healer.

As the scientist that I am, I have studied and learned that mindset techniques could help me get rid of the excruciating pain I was living in, by helping me reframe my identity, beliefs, rules and stories. I looked for a teacher that resonated with me in the realm of mindset, and I happened to find an amazing teacher whose husband is one of the world's most renowned energy healers, taking care of big personalities and movie stars. He got my attention and I enrolled in the $20K certification series that really shifted everything for me, when I combined it with the mindset tools I already had.

All of the sudden it became apparent to me that my entire life and my story had been orchestrated by my soul, so that I could arrive at that moment in time when my desperation to get rid of the pain was so much stronger than the reasons my logical mind could come up with, to stir me out of this unknown path.

As I learned to 'play' with energy which means that I was ferociously practicing all the things that I was given, plus the ones that came to me naturally, many gifts started to be activated within me: psychic abilities, healing modalities, channeling skills, and much more.

The more my heart opened, the more I was able to access

new energy levels and hear my higher self talking to me and guiding me towards exploring the world of energy.

Call me crazy but, since and even now, playing with energy (in other words, doing my energy routine every day) is a non-negotiable item in my daily schedule. That's how much I believe in its transformative power, because that's how it worked for me.

This holistic approach, energy healing, recognizes that we are not just physical beings but also energetic beings, interconnected with the universal energy that flows through us and around us.

If we are connected on social media you will hear me say that what gave me my jaw-dropping transformation so many asked me about wasn't mindset work, and maybe to your surprise wasn't energy healing either, but the combination of both.

And in case you are wondering what energy healing is... It's simply the work energy practitioners like myself do to restore balance and harmony within your body and your field, and raise your frequency and vibration to the point where there is no pain, no guilt, no shame, no physical ailments. And by clearing energetic blockages and rebalancing the flow of energy, you are facilitating a deep sense of relaxation, healing, and emotional release, within you. This is how I healed every single emotional wound and trauma in me and my daughter.

I still remember that afternoon when everything changed. As I was getting my second certification as an energy healer, I needed to find volunteers for healings. Not surprising at all was that as all my gifts were being activated - so were those of my kids. Sofia has been into energy from the very beginning of my journey, maybe because she's called to it too, maybe because she saw how - whatever this was - it was transforming me, or maybe both... But regardless, she was hundred percent open to me doing a healing on her.

I took this opportunity to heal EVERYTHING that needed to be healed between us. It was literally the longest healing I've ever performed and I used every sacred geometry that came to me, including the sacred geometry for total forgiveness.

And YES, if you are thinking about it... there is a sacred geometry for that! - Carmen Benton

I thought I was going in to heal my mistakes, but the healing took me to also heal my mom's and my grandma's karma. It was beautiful, it was powerful. I was crying as I was releasing all of this. I got to the point where I cleared it all: in all timelines, past, present and future, for me, my mom and my grandmother, and I felt this beautiful peace. After the healing was done, we talked and we hugged and I could feel her forgiveness. I've done it.

Now you understand why I'm such a firm believer that energy healing is a profound tool. That's why I invite you to embrace its transformative power, and allow it to dissolve the energetic blockages within you, as it did in myself, and experience the liberation of an open heart that I'm so grateful to be able to experience today.

Highlighting the connection between compassion, forgiveness and personal freedom

60% of the people that have applied to work with me over the last year have said, in their application, that one of the things they would like to get out of our coaching relationship is freedom. This makes me very excited, because I know something they don't. I know that personal freedom is the ultimate destination of the forgiveness journey, and I know the reason they don't feel free is really because they have unresolved trauma that keeps them prisoners of their past. But since healing their trauma is exactly what I help them do, I know that my coaching will absolutely give them the sense of freedom they so much desire.

I have come to realize that freedom is the state of being where you are no longer defined or confined by your past pain and trauma. It is to be able to live fully in the present moment, liberated from the chains of resentment, anger, and victimhood, empowered and able to make conscious choices, follow your passions, and create a life aligned with your values and desires.

With my own experience I can tell you that through forgiveness, personal freedom becomes attainable, because I was literally living in a box, imprisoned by my anger, resentment and fear; but now I'm free, no longer needing external validation and approval, embracing my inherent worthiness and all of who I am. I finally feel the freedom and I know it is about living authentically, expressing your truth, and honoring your unique journey.

I was also able to extend my newfound personal freedom to those around me, by recognizing that their actions and behaviors (triggers) were just a reflection of their own pain and wounds.

Forgiveness and personal freedom are closely intertwined. When you hold on to resentment and refuse to forgive, you remain bound to the pain of the past.

The burden of not forgiving weighs you down, constraining your ability to live fully and authentically. It limits your potential for growth, joy, and meaningful connections with others. In other words, trauma makes you feel the opposite of freedom.

On the other hand, forgiveness sets you free. It liberates you from the grip of negative emotions and allows you to embrace a future filled with possibilities. When you forgive, you release yourself from the role of victim and step into a position of strength and resilience. You regain your power to shape your own life and define your own happiness.

When you embrace forgiveness, you open the door to profound transformation within your relationships. Self-forgiveness is why I was able to rekindle my relationship with my daughter Sofia but, most importantly, with myself. This new freedom allowed me to start seeing life differently and make new empowered decisions towards my future, including finally deciding to follow my passion, fulfill my life's purpose and become a holistic success coach for driven women.

Forgiveness has the power to mend broken bonds, heal emotional wounds, and restore harmony. It allows you to release the weight of resentment, grudges, and past hurts, paving the way for deeper connection and understanding. I'm not attempting to be perceived as Mother Theresa at all, yet I have to say that I still surprise myself with the things and people I've been able to forgive in my life. Lots of pain, lots of intentional vicious hurt towards me from past relationships. None of it matters, it's all water under the bridge because of forgiveness.

I have to say, though, that the act of forgiveness is not for the benefit of others; it is a gift we give ourselves, because by forgiving, we release the toxic energy that keeps us tied to the past. This is how I healed and how you can heal too.

I can definitely tell you from my own experience that I never felt this free until I learned to forgive myself and dropped the chains of guilt, shame, and blame.

The act of forgiveness also holds immense healing potential, not only for yourself but for those you forgive , and sometimes the forgiveness has to go back generations as the traumas and blockages in your energetic body and DNA could have originated centuries of years back; just like I had to do in my own healing journey as well as Sofia's. This is why I say that forgiveness breaks the cycle of pain and allows for the restoration of trust, freedom, and inner peace. It offers the opportunity for all the parties to heal and grow beyond the wounds of the past, paving the way for healthier and more fulfilling relationships.

In closing

Forgiveness is not a one-time event but a continuous journey of self-discovery and growth.

As we come to the end of this chapter, I'd love to invite you to carry the lessons of The Healing Alchemy of Forgiveness with you. Let's remember that we all carry wounds and trauma, and that compassion is a vital component of the healing process. Let's embrace the transformative potential of forgiveness and recognize that personal freedom and empowerment await us on this journey. Let's harness the ripple effect of forgiveness, fostering empathy, compassion, and healing in our relationships and communities.

CARMEN BENTON

Carmen Benton is a retired corporate executive, mom of 3, best selling author and a renowned sought after holistic success coach on a mission to share knowledge that transforms lives by speaking to the heart and truth that resonates with the soul. With her extensive experience and expertise, Carmen empowers high achievers to reach the next level in their lives, relationships, careers, and businesses without burning out. As a professional public speaker and podcast host of the Living Intentionally with Carmen Benton, she shares her deep wisdom on achieving success through inner healing, all without the necessity of reliving past pain. Originally from Panama and now residing in Alaska, Carmen loves traveling, cooking and practicing self-care.

www.carmenbenton.com/links

7

FROM SILENCE TO SOVEREIGNTY: SPINNING SECRETS INTO SACRED WISDOM

BY PAIGE FRISONE

"No one will know the violence it took to become this gentle." - Unknown

Holy. Two things.

One, I write this chapter with both awe and severe humility to have made it this far in life. Because at 30 years young, I hold near and dear the reality that my existence was touch-and-go there for a while and it's time to talk about that.

As a born writer, expressing myself on paper was my lifeline in school, at home, late at night, and first thing in the morning. Today, I deem this chapter my official debut into the world, where beyond writing poems and tormented musings about the point of this thing called life, I'm finally in a position to help people heal by sharing my heart. The bigness of that is not lost on me.

People these days light-heartedly joke about having midlife, even quarter-life crises, but what do you call a life-threatening crisis that seems to have no beginning, no end?

Two, I find it crucial to declare what I know now, unequivocally, which is that you are not your struggle. You are not your diagnosis. You are not here to succumb to the limiting, self-annihilating stories that have successfully, maybe relentlessly, knocked you down time and time again.

What if I told you that the things you perceive to be the absolute worst things about you carry uncontainable wisdom? What if I said that the parts of you that you neglect, repress, suppress, or avoid—whether that's anxiety, depression, panic attacks, or people-pleasing—are not only smart, but are actually dying for your attention?

Whatever parts exist in you that you judge, loathe, wish to change, exist for three predominant reasons: to protect you, keep you safe, and help you survive. We all have parts within us, things about us, that we'd never consciously choose. But knowing their purpose helps ease the pain of it all, I think. Self-understanding opens a door to befriend the shadow, honor it, and maybe even respect it, in time.

And while that can really suck in moments, at this juncture in my life, it's harsh to hate those inner fighters for doing their job. However, I have hated them in the past. Big time. And I was damn good at it. So good, in fact, that I dedicated my entire life to shaming and shrinking them. In doing so, I lost myself and, resultantly, nearly lost my life.

The commitment to obeying my inner abusers became a lifestyle. It created an internal power structure through which I remained chronically subservient to the voices in my head.

The self-loathing dictated what I thought, how I felt, what I 'should' or 'shouldn't' say, what I 'could' or 'couldn't' eat, how I had to dress, my worth (or lack thereof), and other agonizing rules and regs that held me hostage and imprisoned for a decade.

It took me years of detangling this mental construct to realize that whatever it is that we perceive to be 'the problem' is not the problem at all. The parts within me—the anorexia, depression, anxiety, self-harm, and exercise addiction—were all masks, manifestations of something deeper living under the surface.

But by the time I was ready to learn why these parts developed in the first place, I was too far into the addiction of maintaining a particular image, fully convinced of some core flaw and unable to get out.

I quickly discovered that the more I fought to disobey these inner parts, the louder they raged. The only time they hushed was when I listened. When I starved, self-punished, and believed what they told me. The eating disorder and its related minions replaced the four main things that gave me life: family, food, friends, and fun.

I was a hollow shell living tortured inside an invisible war. This was my normal. And from the outside, you would've never known. I took pride in that. I covered up my body with 5X clothing and threw smiles on my face. Like I said, I was good at it.

The eating disorder gave me fleeting breaths of worth and value where I otherwise felt none. I lived on the high of emptiness. Somehow, I remained a top performer in school, extracurricular activities, and whatever other distractions could serve as temporary escapes.

Behind closed doors, my devotion to the eating disorder was sealed through secrets. My life became a gamble, my insides dangling within Dante's hellfire; an unrelenting storm eating me from the inside, awaiting my demise.

I held on. I held on. Thank all the powers that be, I held on.

Through the life experiences I'll share with you here, you'll see that I've lived on both ends of contrast: light and dark, health and disease, life and death. I've found that existing on this planet is ironic and gut-wrenching and stunning and miraculous, and sometimes all at once. I invite you to suit up, strap in, do whatever you have to do to enjoy the ride.

It's worth it.

I can say now that healing is, without a doubt, non-linear, complex, and humbling as ever. I still look back in awe of it all. At times, I still face the pits. But it's different now. Because I'm different.

Still, much of my life is fragmented, non-chronological, enigmatic, and confusing, which may be reflected here with intention. At 30 years young, I have lived lifetimes of pain and, resultantly, carry infinite depth and insight. We all do.

At long last, I live to tell the tale of having unlocked, unleashed, and unearthed the truth that has patiently awaited me all this time.

This is my story.

The Revolving Door

"I am experiencing discouragement to such a degree that I wonder what could ever help me. I have an unconscious desire to 'disappear' in order to bother the people around me as little as possible. I therefore permanently reject myself. This can go as far as self-hate that leads me to punish and destroy myself." - The Complete Dictionary of Ailments and Diseases, Jacques Martel.

I remember sitting in eating disorder treatment for the umpteenth time, age 24, only to be told that I am a miracle. I laughed, rolled my eyes, and huffed and puffed this truth away. At this point, and for ten years prior, I had been committed to blowing my one home—this body—down.

You couldn't have convinced me that the sky was blue because all I saw was black. My countless teams of behavioral health techs told me to be grateful I exist, but their encouragement lost to the strength of my belief system: that I was a burden and, therefore, such was life.

I hyperfixated on my perceived flaws and would do anything to fix them. This commitment to self-correction has since propelled me into a business dedicated to helping others rewire and not fall victim to everything they think.

Let it be known that no one wants to suffer. Pain is never a conscious choice. It took me years into my recovery to validate that I was not choosing to starve or die, regardless of the voices that overtly told me to. These were desperate attempts to survive in the best and only way I knew how. Sometimes, in resignation lives the strongest plea.

10 years of life spent in and out of treatment centers, barely alive, hardly surviving. Not eating, not sleeping, not here. Hopping from one level of care to another—24-hour facilities, to partial hospitalizations, to intensive outpatients—it felt easier to go through the motions of life with other wounded souls than braving it on my own. Outside of treatment, my life, for unknown reasons, was a fast track to lifelessness.

Being guided through my days temporarily filled a gaping wound that lived, unbearably, at my core. It really did take a village.

I longed for safety, stability, and answers. I met these needs in backwards ways; through sterile, monitored environments. I became an observer of my own life, thinking my way through fracture, watching time pass until pain would end.

My treatment friends and I followed a strict, minute-to-minute program. Scheduled meals, scheduled outings, scheduled emotional processing times. We'd wake up at 6:30 AM to load up the caravan and arrive for vital checks by eight. Staff checked heart rate, labs, weight, and blood pressure on the regular. Our supervised breakfasts, the first dreaded time of day, was 8:30 AM sharp.

From here, a classic day involved various group therapies

and skills groups, supervised lunch, individual therapy, one-on-ones with your psychiatrist or dietician, then supervised dinner. Shower, rinse, repeat. I'd live in treatment for weeks to months at a time, depending on insurance coverages and the intensity of the relapses. I literally lost the ability to do life on my own.

Some days, I felt like my best self here. I had emotional support, validation, and the comfort of eating amongst people who understood. Other days, I rebelled and grew disturbingly non-compliant. I broke rules. I got kicked out of some centers for self-negligence and self-harm. I began to learn that treatment wasn't just a one-and-done like I expected it to be. I grew deeper in over my head, increasingly more afraid of my mind.

What do you do when your vices stop working? Where do you turn when your safe place isn't anymore? I constantly spun my wheels. Judged myself for every choice. Even when I wanted to change, I didn't know how. Other times, I thought I wanted to change but actually didn't. I shamed myself for feeling life was this hard, which only made things worse.

This was when I began to learn that there are true repercussions for not loving yourself. I'd lost privileges to living my life unsupervised. Then, I lost privileges to living a supervised life. I toggled again on both ends, working further to think myself out of sickness.

Underneath the facade, I was crumbling. I succumbed to those inescapable inner voices. They probed, What's wrong with you? Why can't you just feel better? Figure it out. The more I tried, the harder life got. So I returned to my way of filtering life's intensity—through restricting and more exercise.

It's incredible, the mental gymnastics. I lived on edge, always about to implode.

I will say that behavioral intervention saved my life numerous times and for that, I am forever grateful. But beyond the short-term care, the long-term impact of treatment (for me) was completely unsustainable. It kept me alive for short spurts as I cycled through the system on repeat, until it finally clicked. The one blaring lesson that changed everything: No one was coming to save me.

Don't get me wrong. I met plenty of people throughout these experiences that genuinely changed my life. And I thought that by receiving intensive care, I was doing everything I possibly could to get better. But my default behaviors remained unchanged.

As much as I fought this truth, I did eventually learn that you can't think your way out of feeling, nor can you think your way into lasting change (without behavioral change). As the saying goes, "Nothing changes if nothing changes."

I fibbed about the intensity of my behaviors with my nutritionist, but she knew the truth once I stepped on the scale. I was dazed by distortion and manipulated hunger cues, not able to tell the difference between feeling empty and full. I struggled to be honest about what took place behind closed doors. It was like the scale had the power to reveal my innermost secrets, without me even knowing the actual number.

The lines between reality and imagination, dreamtime and waking state, blurred. Boundaries grew non-existent. I pushed myself to edges I didn't even know I had. I stopped sleeping for months at a time. I was a walking liability. I experienced some mania. You couldn't change my mind or its mission.

Needless to say, I walked in and out of treatment centers more desperate than the time prior. Nothing changed, nothing sustained. I felt more and more like a failure. I blamed myself. The cycle continued.

I'd weight restore, relapse, weight restore, relapse. After my last attempt at treatment, back in 2017, I was forced to stop relying on non-sustaining systems. In a way, this left me on my own with myself; the exact thing I had been running from all these years. In hindsight, this was the greatest gift.

Luckily, by now, I had all the tools in my toolbelt. I learned mindfulness techniques. I did meditation. I studied trauma in school. I was well-versed in Cognitive Behavioral Therapy (CBT), Dialectical Behavior Therapy (DBT), Acceptance and Commitment Therapy (ACT), and countless other therapeutic constructs.

I knew how to titrate thought patterns, ground the body, compartmentalize. I knew when I succumbed to black and white (linear) thinking. I knew how to practice radical acceptance, using the wise mind...on and on.

Needless to say, I was smart. We all are. We're smart in the ways we choose to survive and we're smart in the ways we know better. But that's seldom enough to make sustainable change. Why?

After countless times through this revolving door, I started wondering why the interventions I received in treatment were short-lived. I had heard the term 'lifer' from my time there; it's used to describe someone who returns every couple of months. Lifers are those who spend more time in treatment than out of it.

I knew these people. They became their eating disorder. Their identity was their illness. The fact that this term even existed pissed me off. I felt stuck inside this system, juggling the worse of two evils: life inside these walls or life outside of them.

On any given day, it was a toss-up. I had subconsciously created a co-dependency with the treatment world and, resultantly, with the eating disorder identity. I forgot who I was without it, which reinforced my need for it. I sought a pass from facing reality and somehow created a sub-reality that kept me safe in an illusory way.

Observing the role I played in my life was the first step to shifting the energy around it. Taking accountability for both my conscious and subconscious choices was a huge pill to swallow at first.

So much damage had been done, but at the end of my rope, I had to face the music. I worked to identify what, specifically, wasn't working for me in my current approach to recovery and why. This shift in attention alone forced me to think more critically. It gave me more agency than operating on autopilot.

After exhausting my options in self-destruction, I was curious about what lived on the other side. Maybe things would be easier. It was worth a shot.

The Emergency

"Anorexia...is an attempt to make my inner void die of hunger and make it so small that it will disappear and will no longer demand anything at all." - The Complete Dictionary of Ailments and Diseases, Jacques Martel.

I was fifteen when I declared our household the 'House of Silence.' No one spoke. Truth lived below the surface...in felt senses, interpretations, what wasn't said and therefore known.

Silence was survival.

The only way for my family to remain a family was to not acknowledge the twelve-ton elephant in the room—my parents' impending divorce.

I've always been amazed by how much gets communicated in the in-between. I became fluent in silence, the nuanced passive-aggression, the telepathy that comes. My intuition had never been stronger, the inner war never worse.

I went to school to cry about home, went home to cry about school. Every moment delicate, unstable.

Mundane tasks were the hardest, the simple things, the most obscure. Getting to and from, answering questions, chewing food...

I constantly felt as though I needed to hit 'pause' on life to digest what had already happened. But life kept moving, so I spun out trying to stay caught up. I now know my environments were not conducive to my sensitivity. I felt bulldozed by sensory experiences: movies, office lights, fragrance, words. I blamed myself for this, unable to adapt to an impossibly loud world.

While divorce may have been an obvious next step for some, it was my family's blindspot. We lived in the liminal. The indefinite. The gray. At least under the same roof, we could keep pretending.

Inevitably, the levee broke. My parents never fought until that night. But just as Sir Isaac Newton's third law of motion claims that every action has an equal and opposite reaction, silence too-long suppressed spews words like daggers straight into bones.

Dad shattered the ice in the room with his sharpness:

We are not a family. Just five separate people living under the same roof.

Hearing these words, Earth as I knew it may as well have crumbled beneath my feet.

That was it.

The end of the 18-Year Illusion.

He said it. We all knew it. No one could bear it.

Mom supported the sentiment. She condensed that which lived on her bitten tongue for years into one compact sentence.

Love is no longer the binding force of this marriage, but you. The kids.

Us. The kids.

I sat still, numb, watching the bubbling truths erupt from volcanic floors to form our new forever. Another cracked chip in another monstrous iceberg.

I wrote a poem about this night. Poetry brings what lives below the surface in inexplicable ways, to light:

Family
To force words of bones
Pulled, ripped & wrung.

To divvy / the arms / of a starfish
One for you, you,
Ossicles, family particles,
Sprawled.
Every|one | pieced in five
We are islands.
Oh, how
We've drifted such length,
Such distance.

This was the day the hopeless romantic in me simply became hopeless. It's what I brought up in treatment over and over again, unable to reconcile such grief. The magnitude of silence throughout my life, all that wasn't said, but known, broke me.

So I lost my appetite for life. For years and to no avail, I worked to unravel my life in retrospect.

Worse before Better

"I have the impression that my survival depends upon my capacity to cut myself off from others. By being as thin as possible, I will no longer be visible; I will disappear from sight and hide to be safe." - The Complete Dictionary of Ailments and Diseases, Jacques Martel.

For my first few treatment stays, I was convinced that if my parents could reconcile their relationship, I would recover with ease. Ha.

In treatment, family therapy is an integral part of the curriculum. As we don't heal in isolation, educating loved ones about eating disorders, triggers, coping skills, and support at home is crucial for re-entry.

That's what I wanted...a healthy home. Not one that

presented as tame on the outside while our insides were screaming.

We were a sound but secretive unit, the only ones who truly knew, but could never quite explain, the gravity of the situation.

I wanted parents who lived as happily as the tales of their karmic love story promised. But, instead, I found myself clever and ill, working to break free from the entrapment of home, silence, the mind.

I thought that if I could just keep everything tidy, everyone harmonious, my world wouldn't fall apart. Instead, I lost my freaking mind.

It turns out that when suppressed for long enough, emotions come out sideways. I was able to hide much of my struggle away at university, only letting the truth seep out when family came to visit. I remember select moments from Thanksgiving, 2012: anorexia's least favorite holiday.

My family greeted me on campus in Indianapolis, Indiana with sheer terror. I knew I didn't look the same as I did when they last saw me, but dysmorphic eyes kept me from knowing what, exactly, they saw. I hid under long, heavy sweaters that mimicked how I felt inside. I wore agony on my sleeve, not able to partake in family meals or pleasantries without sickness showing.

My life was suddenly on the clock. By this point, my EKGs were irregular and my heart was close to caving. My eyes were dark, my skin pale, and yet anorexia convinced me I wasn't ever thin enough and therefore, unworthy of care. I turned a blind eye to the repercussions.

If my family hadn't intervened, I don't know that I would've made it.

So I withdrew from school at my lowest weight and at peak madness. It was an all-hands-on-deck moment. Everyone kicked into survival mode to get me admitted. Thank you, family.

When I stepped onto that plane, at the age of 19, for treatment across the country, Mom fell into a deep depression. My inner world now uncontainable, my secrets seeped out and onto loved ones. I couldn't bear seeing the impact of my pain on others for two reasons.

For one, I'm super sensitive. Like, uber sensitive. So, as much as I hurt myself, I would never, ever wish to hurt another. Let alone my nearest and dearest.

Second, the impact of this life-threatening issue forced me to see that I mattered. And that regardless of my attempts to control (my thoughts, feelings, relationships), family became indirectly yet inextricably linked to my process.

Thus began the long way back home to myself. Therapist after therapist asked me about family messaging, generational patterns, childhood trauma...anything to help explain it all. I found myself getting lost in rabbit holes late at night, searching for answers, only to come up short and wrapped around the tiresome question, why?

Alas, family secrets came out through the grapevine in pieces. I grew well-versed in the family narrative. I knew that my closest aunt had a lifelong struggle with the restrict-binge-purge cycle and a paralyzing body image. And that she had been shipped off as a kid by her mom, my Nana, to what my aunt calls a weight-reducing 'fat camp.'

These words still make me cringe.

I knew that my aunt eventually had life-altering weight reduction surgeries and that my great aunt—Nana's sister—had numerous, non-sustaining weight-reduction procedures as well. Bands in the belly, gastric sleeves, you name it.

Anything to just feel better.

Nana was a chronic dieter, caving for mere spoons of whipped cream once in a blue moon. When you saw her, she'd comment on not just her own weight gain or loss, but yours too.

She wanted you to eat, but would comment on both when

you did and didn't. Having weight on your body was a character defect. Beyond the food, appearance was everything.

Somehow, Nana declared me as the 'thin one' in my youth, passing a beauty contest I never knew I entered. Regardless of her assessment of me, however, I never had a sustainable 'in.' I was 16 when she first told me to get a nose job.

Though Mom worked to be different from Nana, the apple didn't fall far from the tree. I grew up around preoccupations with healthy food, black-and-white thinking, and elimination diets. Inevitably, I became preoccupied too.

I thought my eating disorder came out of nowhere, that it was simply a 'me' problem. Don't get me wrong. It is. No two struggles are the same. All diagnoses, dis-order, and dis-ease are deeply personal and show up for different reasons. But there are shared threads amongst the collective, too.

Turns out my family lineage comes laced with tides of self-loathing, low self-esteem, conditional love, and an overt struggle to accept oneself fully.

These days, I treat generational patterns as wise connectors. The root traumas of my life have directly taught me about my ancestors, giving me information I never would've otherwise known.

But what do we do with this information? How do we change the programs? Because regardless of genetics and inherited generational trauma, there are always counter-narratives. In this case, these would be epigenetics and generational growth.

As I excavated my family history, I saw more darkness, more tangled knots at first. I longed for this fight to amount to something. Maybe then, I could deem it all—life—worthwhile.

This no longer felt like just my war to win.

The Cave

"Anorexia is basically my need to fill an inner void of affective nourishment. I need the unconditional Love and acceptance of my inner mother." - The Complete Dictionary of Ailments and Diseases, Jacques Martel.

It wasn't until Nana passed that I started connecting with her in ways that weren't possible in the physical world. In the non-physical, I could return to doing what I do best: feeling between the lines.

I think of her when I see amethyst (her birthstone), or any expression of 222 (her birthday). I call on her for guidance and know she forever holds the respectable role of matriarch in our family.

No one could replace Nana, but I grew more curious about how her energy would be reallocated. As the law of energy states, energy cannot be created or destroyed, only converted to a different form.

She passed in December 2018. Nana walked into the hospital in her full face of makeup, as poised and beautiful as ever, only to not return home again that evening.

That following February, she would've had a birthday, on 2/22. I was in my last semester of college, a process that's forever tainted with memories of, once again, brutal means of survival. More entrapments of the mind.

Two schools, two withdrawals, and close to six years later, I received my degree in English Literature, Creative Writing, and Contemplative Psychology.

It wasn't until this final semester, just a few months without Nana, when my life truly changed forever. The short version of the story is that I went cold turkey off all my meds. I highly recommend not doing that.

The truer version of this story is that I experienced sheer divine intervention; an experience that doesn't make sense to the linear, conscious mind, only to that of the soul.

By now, I had studied diverse healing practices involving Western medicine, Eastern medicine, integrative care, holistic health, and trauma.

Between my studies and all I'd learned from a decade in treatment, something wasn't adding up. I became acutely aware of the subconscious repercussions to taking these pills every day.

Every time I opened the bottles, prepped the chemical cocktail in my hands, I felt shame, confusion, fear, and judgment.

I was on anxiety medication, antidepressants, and mood stabilizers. Plus, thyroid medication and IBS medication, treating manifested repercussions of the eating disorder. I had been diagnosed and misdiagnosed. Deemed enigmatic, strange.

I had pills to treat the side effects of other pills alongside and no substantial evidence to support the why.

Eventually, my conflicting relationship with these pills became more harmful than my taking them. I grew indifferent before I grew angry.

At this point, I truly was, as they say, sick and tired of being sick and tired. More so, I grew sick and tired of being perceived this way by others and, more dangerously, myself.

This was the moment, holding these pills, where I wondered, What if I just don't? My patterns of non-compliance in treatment flashed in my mind like a montage. This was the first time I considered if this behavior was my intuition working adamantly to get my attention.

So I didn't refill the scripts. And I didn't think about it much until about a week later. But I did, obviously, become a liability to my psychiatrist. Our relationship ended. And I went into what I like to call The Cave for the next two weeks.

Life was a blur. Black, dense, heavy, and dark. I went

through the motions of life, showing up for class dazed and out of it, tolerating.

This withdrawal experience wasn't much different from how I had known life to be, anyway. But this time, I could feel the outcome might be different. I had a hunch I might be free from something. I didn't know what, but I was sure as heck ready to figure it out.

For perhaps the first time in my life, I could hear my authentic self fighting to push through the layered cracks of concrete. Stubbornness and pervasive curiosity motivated me to see this through. I became my own science experiment.

I came out of The Cave on Nana's birthday that year, just a few months before graduation. Inexplicably, I knew that she helped me through this transition.

The fog lifted. Brain chemistry rebalanced (in time). And I became certain that this moment was truly the beginning of the rest of my life.

The Emergence

"It is not an error that you have been born a sensitive human being with a tender nervous system and a heart that is sometimes broken. Inside the wound, a spiral. The tenderness there, the shakiness, the grief...not an error to be remedied or cured...but a doorway to essence, a portal to life." - Matt Licata, Psychotherapist and Author.

I'll never forget when one of my college professors said, Sometimes, the answers are in the questions, which was lucky, given that my entire life was exactly that—a question. As you can likely see by now, I'd be hard-pressed to locate just one defining moment of my life, as who I am now has been defined by a series of transformative inductions.

Writing this, I'm nearly five years medication-free and it has been by far one of the best decisions of my life. Two years ago, I reclaimed yet another decade of my life that was formerly blacked out. Ages three-13. Let's go there.

My whole adult life, I lived without any chronological memory, only echoes of versions of me told by family in fragments; always subject to others' (mis)perceptions. I never had the embodied ability to confirm or deny any events of my life.

Up until recently, I wasn't able to know how vulnerable this made me feel; powerless and without agency. Without medication and without an active eating disorder to suppress it all, everything starts to bubble up to the surface. Sometimes, it floods. This has been the ultimate recalibration, bravely learning how to more directly experience life.

On this particular night two years ago, I laid in bed to rest. As my brain transitioned into theta waves, I flashed to a jarring memory: a childhood secret that I instantly realized I was still, unknowingly, keeping. I found it odd that after a life of therapy (starting age seven), I had something inside me that I'd never said out loud.

As a Subconscious Health Practitioner, I treat memories like gems, clues. They take us to the moments when we couldn't metabolize our environment, down to the exact sensory experience. These sensations get stuck in the cells.

I'd heard stories of people accessing repressed memories through modes like EMDR (Eye Movement Desensitization and Reprocessing) or brainspotting, both subconscious healing methods. I never figured something like this could happen to me.

In my practice, I guide clients struggling with depression, anxiety, addiction, and trauma to heal the unprocessed, subconsciously stored memories—whether from childhood, past lives, and/or generations—that signal present-day patterns of stress and dis-ease. This was yet another moment in my professional career where I was challenged to follow my own advice, taste my own medicine.

The way in which I received these memories was like that of a simulation. As though the star of A Christmas Carol, I was taken by a guiding entity to re-meet and re-greet every past version of me.

I was shown my preschool building first; something I hadn't remembered since being there. From there, kindergarten, and then, each subsequent year of my life up until high school.

The guiding force asked one question each step of the way: What else do you remember? What else do you remember? I answered calmly, filling in the blanks with details of each classroom, times at recess, outfits, haircuts, my peers...

I accessed an entire archived file of my life, documented with data. Thoughts I thought, feelings I felt. What was previously blurry became clear, like binoculars finally in focus.

There it was. My innate wisdom, unleashed. It was an epic, long overdue, self-reunion.

As my black-and-white life filled with color, I hit the glacier I formerly couldn't and wouldn't have seen. It sent chills down my spine. At long last, I found the missing piece of the puzzle. The answer every previous therapist I'd ever seen had been waiting for.

Repressed sexual trauma. Discovered at age 27.

F*ck.

If you learned there was more to the story of your life that could help explain why you are the way you are, how would that impact you? For me, this was a monumental, severely disruptive moment.

All of my maladaptive ways started to make sense. The anorexia's attempt to help me disappear and control the uncontrollable. The limiting beliefs of feeling innately wrong and unworthy of love and care. The struggles that showed up repeatedly in relationships, my mind, sexuality, body image, on and on...

Any other time in my life, I would've tucked this secret away with the rest. But I decided to do the opposite. In eating disorder recovery, we're taught to follow 'opposite action,' meaning, doing the next right thing even when you don't want to. Even if it straight-up blows.

It's important to note that my tolerance for secrets at this point in my life was (and still is) non-existent. So whatever feels stuck or tucked away deep within the confines of shame, I run towards them. I treat sharing secrets like working muscles; terrifying when new or atrophied, easier with consistent reps.

So I brought this one to therapy.

Thankfully, I saw her the day after having this revelation. I grew antsy watching the clock tick until 2 PM. That's my favorite time. Up until then, work didn't matter. Therapy was my focus; it's my unwavering safe place. It connects me with the wholeness of me from childhood to adulthood, past to now.

The time came (finally) to walk into her office, my sanctuary. The diffuser was on as it usually was, effervescing eucalyptus into the air, reminding me of my nighttime aromatherapy rituals as a kid.

I looked around, greeting the plants and stones internally, tracking what may have changed since the last time we connected. I read the energy as I always do, interpreting the subtleties below the surface. I sat calmly, cautiously, staring at the blowing, geometric tapestries moments before greeting her. It was a crisp, sunny day.

I smiled. Asked how she was. I like knowing what's going on with her. Though I couldn't retain much mentally, I was also a pro at operating on empty. I worked to ground into her words, to slow down time.

After our check-in, I leapt right at the elephant in the room. My words were clumsy, like a newborn just learning to walk:

So I remembered a thing that happened. I'm not sure what you'll think of it or if it matters at all...I've never shared it with anyone and never thought I would...

She invited me deeper into this moment with an embodied calm unlike anything I've ever known. I let the caged bird out, stopping to breathe after every few words.

He had me make out with him. He turned it into a game. I hated it. I remember pools. Role play. Upstairs, in the shower. Downstairs, in the basement. Sneaking around. For years. Secrets.

I sat to catch my breath as I anxiously awaited her response. My heart pounded, heat waves rushing through my face just like when I was young. For the first time, I could affirm now that this was what it felt like back then to be triggered. I had these exact reactions growing up and never knew why. I faulted myself for having them. Hushed them away.

Between various traumas in life, coupled with years of medication and an eating disorder, it can be challenging to decipher triggers from non-triggers when all you feel is chaos. My body and mind have ensued more disorientation than I can comfortably comprehend.

I was so preoccupied with being 'found out' when I was young. I was constantly on guard, hypervigilant. Any time anything sex-related was mentioned, I panicked and fled the scene. I was embarrassed, ashamed, and constantly confused—at school, with friends, watching TV. I had to make my life smaller and smaller to find safety, spiraling me into an inner war that in hindsight, makes perfect sense.

I knew something was wrong then, but I was too busy surviving. Too busy protecting him. "He'd never hurt me," I convinced myself. I was always told 'family first,' so I never thought to question it. I was willing to take this to my grave. I promised myself I would. My life is evidence of that. Thus began the secret-keeping.

The density of the silence in therapy this day was suffocating, but I knew this feeling well by now. I anxiously thought to myself, "Please say something."

Wow. She paused.

Not only is this a huge deal, Paige, but it makes total sense.

Breathe. Breathe. Breathe.

Have you ever taken inventory of your secrets? Of the ways you create order from chaos?

Upon examining the role of our secrets, addictions, or the ways we protect ourselves, we defuse them. From there, we can respect them. And from there, maybe even befriend them.

May the deepest healing commence. Breathe.

The Light

"What you seek is seeking you."
Rumi

Two years ago, I discovered the missing link in my story, and I'm still healing from it. From a lot of things, really. There is information within me tucked away that I'm still eager to encounter in due time. It's my job to take care of myself, to prepare my body, my home, to honor that information when it comes through.

I've learned to trust and respect the non-linearity of healing, knowing my inner wisdom is always available, no matter what state I'm in.

As the common phrase goes, "What happened to you is not your fault, but the healing is your responsibility." Luckily, I've dedicated myself to what spiritual master Abraham Hicks would call the 'bring it on life.'

No matter how much fear I experience in life, I will always run straight to it to get through it. This is where my strength and sovereignty live.

Today, I find myself devoted to upping my standard for life. I geek out about the invisible and unseen. I'm here to swim in the depths and to know them. I am my own client, therapist, student, teacher, child, parent, doctor, healer, and absolute best friend. I've worked hard to prove this to myself. And there's no turning back from this knowing.

My life as it stands is a walking study of nature and nurture, genetics and epigenetics, the conscious and subconscious, science and spirit, the personal and transpersonal...and the inquiry behind how all of these pieces fit together to create the mosaic of our beingness.

This work is required of my soul, in all of life's initiations, to find what self-sustaining health and wellness truly looks like, all the while honoring that we are all, always, works in progress. I've learned that the deepest gift we can give one another is to trust the wisdom of our unique journeys and support each other through them.

As you've likely seen throughout my story, sometimes, we must cycle through the same resistance hundreds of times before shifting the trajectory. These lessons aren't pleasant but they're oh, so valuable. I can now affirm what I never believed to be true before now: it really does get better. Better yet, it gets to be amazing.

After acquiring certification for subconscious healing a few years ago, it was transformational enough in my life to launch a business about it. It is my purpose to help people know that we're designed to heal. That's a fact. Whatever's getting in the way of knowing, that's the work.

It took me time to pick myself up by the bootstraps. My experiences have shown me why it's not always the case that when you know better, you do better. Knowing something in your mind isn't always enough to shift dominant, reflexive thoughts, patterns, or behaviors. Healing isn't a matter of intellectual prowess.

So, if you're anything like me and have felt as though you've tried it all—you've read the books, you've listened to the podcasts, you've spent the money, you've done the courses, you're tired of talking about it, and you don't know where to turn—where do you go?

In. We go deeper in. I wouldn't recommend going there alone, however. At least not at first. Let's resource up, cultivate your professional team, then dip our toes in those bubbling waters together. I'd love nothing more than to be a part of your journey and I'm excited for you to see what's on the other side.

As Carl Jung states, "Until you make the unconscious conscious, it will direct your life and you will call it fate." To this I say, don't let your wounds become your fate. Regardless of the mental distress, the societal messaging, the family norms, and trauma, you are here to heal.

You don't have to know how yet. But if you need more or different support in navigating these aches, I'm here for you. It's so cool to be able to be here for you, because it reaffirms that I am also here for me. Finally.

I'm also grateful to report that I'm the healthiest and happiest I've ever been. I'm not anorexic, addicted, self-harming, depressed, anxious, or medicated. I am, however, very human, which means I have those inner fighters that show up on occasion to show me what else needs to heal. I welcome them.

This is the realistic, non-linear dance of healing. And it doesn't mean I can't also strive to have an awesome life. Because I have, in fact, built that. Moreso, I expect it. And I deserve it.

So do you.

Sometimes, I catch myself speeding up or overcompensating, in a rat-race with myself to operate for 'lost time'. Then I remember there's no such thing. That's merely a default program, a perception, a limiting belief.

Everything has unfolded perfectly. Trusting this has been a

process. And sure, I have my work cut out for me, still. But I'm here for it.

Why?

Because I owe it to myself to live fully for the past parts of me that almost didn't. I owe it to myself to look in the mirror and love who I see because I've worked too hard to not feel this way.

As the common phrase goes, "You didn't come this far to only come this far." Life really is too short for that. We've all suffered enough, don't you think?

If nothing else, I wish for you to turn this page feeling that it's all possible. Whatever you desire to heal, you can heal. It's your design. Don't let anyone tell you otherwise. Don't settle for less.

Know that you hold the steering wheel. Your life is in direct relationship to your limiting beliefs. Your body is in direct relationship with your mind. You have more power within you than you may consciously ever know. Discovering this is dancing with magic.

I never thought I'd be here today to share this story. But just as I've learned there are repercussions for not loving ourselves, I've found there are also rewards for doing so. I deem this one of them.

It remains my honor to help you traverse through and transmute your painful unknowns into pure joy and glory. We will wade through the muck until you remember your ancient, infinite wisdom. I witness these light bulbs go off with clients daily and it never fails to amaze me. The ripple effect of healing is contagious. Heal yourself, heal the world.

There is wisdom in secret-keeping. But there is greater wisdom in releasing. The choice is yours. You are the light you seek. I'm simply here to help you prove it.

PAIGE FRISONE

Paige Frisone is a Subconscious Health Practitioner, Professional Writer, and Award-Winning Impact Speaker stationed in Colorado. She is the founder and owner of her integrative healing practice, Inner Realm Wellness LLC, where she helps men and women around the globe struggling with depression, anxiety, trauma, and addiction heal on a cellular and therefore sustainable level.

Paige is certified in a healing technology that incorporates over 14+ modalities from Eastern and Western medicine combined to help people live a life of optimal, self-regenerative health and wellness. She received her degree in English Literature / Creative Writing and Contemplative Psychology and uses a transpersonal lens in her practice.

Through her podcast episodes, published articles, 1:1 client sessions, and digital presence, Paige is committed to helping people unlock their infinite potential, live by their wisdom, and know that we are all designed to heal.

In her free time, she enjoys moving in nature, soaking up the sun, and letting intuition lead.

www.innerrealmwellness.life/links

8

THE JOKER'S JUGGLE

BY KATRINA MARSH

Growing up, I was entranced by the captivating act of a juggler, skillfully maneuvering objects in a mesmerizing display of coordination and balance. Little did I know that I would unwittingly adopt the role of the juggler in my own life, using busyness and work as my props. Like a joker performing tricks to distract from vulnerability, I would immerse myself in a whirlwind of activities.

From a young age, I eagerly embarked on various entrepreneurial ventures. From lemonade stands to dog walking, raking leaves off my neighbors' lawns, and just about any other problem I could find a solution for and provide to my neighborhood of customers. I stepped into the jester's shoes with each role I took, carrying the act with me as I portrayed my skill set of the day, to the audience of my choosing. Would it be my neighbor, Dana, and her Pomeranians that I serve today? Or maybe the thirsty afternoon joggers looking for a refreshment?

The reward of a dollar here and fifty cents there is definitely motivating for any young kid realizing the payoff of their hard work. However, more than the jingling of coins or a crisp bill, the recognition and pride of facilitating my own route to success was really what fueled my passion for problem-solving in the form of entrepreneurial endeavors. The recognition and admiration of my audiences ignited my drive to continue the act.

Though, it wasn't until later on that I realized my hard working habits were an act. At the time I was just doing more of what made me feel good. Being around people while having projects to do and tasks to complete gave me purpose.

For a long time, I was on a search for this purpose. In times of chaos and distress I went into learned and adopted overworking habits and then into fits of burnout, just to repeat the cycle over and over again. I kept looking outside of myself to see what problems needed solving and where I could be of use to others. But you cannot pour from an empty cup.

You cannot serve others effectively without first understanding yourself.

The Jester's Daughter

I remember going door to door with business cards my Papa had made for me.

Katrina Enterprises, No Job Too Small

Think back to when you were younger. What did you want to be when you grew up? If you can remember, were they the professions your parents held? Was it a mixture of different things that intrigued you - like a zookeeping ballerina?

The things that excited me as a child were endless and what I wanted to be, was indirectly influenced by my busy bee parents. My oh-so official business cards just about summed me up at this point. I wanted to be everything when I grew up, No Job Too Small.

My mother was a devoted homemaker, and me and my crew of siblings were no small job. Kristen Marsh was made for motherhood though. If you had asked her what she wanted to be when she grew up, she would've shown you her collection of babydolls and told you, "I want to be a mom". She was amazing at it. Balancing dance recitals, little league games, packed lunches, and church on Sundays. There were 4 of us Marsh-lings, and we kept her quite busy.

The root of the Joker's spirit however, was undoubtedly inherited by my father. His tireless work ethic served as an unseen jester's hat upon his head. My father is, in all sense of the word, a workaholic. The dedication and commitment to his craft painted the backdrop of my upbringing, creating a structured and disciplined family unit. My father, Michael Marsh, specializes in the Emergency Medical Services industry, and the amount of unbelievably gripping and harrowing stories I was told throughout my life by him, could fill up volumes of their own. You would think he had the easiest job in the world, the way he effortlessly juggles his career, family, and social life now. The way he could naturally react and function, within each intense state of emergency he responded to. This skill set was anything but natural though, and that now-perfected balance was hard-earned and came at a high cost.

My father's deep devotion to his work led him to many incredible opportunities, but his acquired ability to stay functional in disastrous settings came at a toll to his mental health. The desensitization of seeing that day's circus of a crime scene allowed him to exponentially grow in his career, always preparing for the next trauma-inducing call.

Whether it was his Blackberry, radio, or pager, when it dinged he was ready to run out the door to aid in that day's disaster. From a child's standpoint, this drilled the idea of work-above-all into my young mind. As an amazing father figure, it is clear that this was never his intention although it did make sense to me on a subconscious level. When you find your passion, you put your all into it. Although this mindset can be a healthy motivator in certain lenses, the overdrive he went into for years, for the sake of his career, led him to hard lessons. My father eventually had to work equally as hard to earn back what he had lost, learn to protect his soul, and find the necessary balance. And, as my father's stubborn daughter, this would be a lesson that I would need to learn myself as well.

The Juggler's Mask

My inspired work ethic followed me as I ventured into academia. The Joker within me found new props to juggle. Books, assignments, and extracurricular activities became additional pins added to my act. The audience I performed for was now prospective colleges, administrative figures, and scholarship grantors, and their awe was hard to achieve. I gave it my all and was rewarded with a spot in some of my top schools, scholarships from the majority of which I applied, and achievements, honors, and awards that followed me into my graduation ceremony.

Yet, I still had feelings of discontent and sought out the next venture. In what I thought was an unwavering pursuit of my goals, I unexpectedly found myself in a long-term and turbulent relationship.

I began to drift from my goals, however, my relentless overworking habits remained unaffected. As a waitress at the time, I dedicated myself to long days and weeks, juggling additional roles as a tutor and personal assistant, all while attending classes at two, local community colleges. Amidst these commitments, I managed to divert my attention from my ex-partner's infidelity.

As I look back on the relationship between me and my ex-partner, I realize we were both still trying to figure out our lives and the people that we were or wanted to be. Both young, curious, and restless beings. We took different approaches to these feelings, but I have long let go of any bottled up resentment, both having made mistakes as we grew closer and closer to our inevitable end.

I did not realize I had been gradually growing accustomed to this fast and hard way of our relationship. I started to expect the turbulence and dissociated more and more from each situation that arose. I was unrecognizable to myself. Becoming more of a drone than a human as I lost sensitivity and overworked in place of dealing with the problems at hand. I toiled diligently to maintain the façade of a flourishing relationship to the public, family, and friends.

I lacked the capacity to share deep feelings with others. I am lucky to have had the opportunity and the people willing to have worked with me through tough life chapters, as there are many people who don't have this support. My mother, sister, and friends would have absolutely lent their ear to my grievances, but it was me who did not allow myself to access that vulnerable side. I personally stopped myself from sharing such details at the risk of looking like I did not have it all together. These instances were where my workaholic behaviors really prevailed, allowing me to consume my time and thoughts with work and school so I did not feel the need to dwell on personal hurdles or emotional triggers.

Workaholism is seemingly an acceptable addiction in our society. The 'grind' culture of paying your dues now so you can enjoy life later, paradoxically promotes a lower quality of life overall. You may not even realize it, but by putting work as your main priority you are neglecting other major areas of your personal life. The work you are doing for others whether it's your business or your boss is, most times, directly taking away from the work you can be putting into yourself. That is why this idea of a work-life balance is so important and something to be implemented as soon as possible.

If I were to put just as much work into getting to know myself as I was distracting myself from hardship, the growth could have been exponential. The professional and personal successes could have been simultaneous instead of one or the other.

Instead, the distraction of work gave me small but instant gratification and I fed from that. With each bump I experienced with my ex-partner, the painted Joker's mask became thicker as I tried to hide the internal struggles I experienced. The jester's nature remained embedded within me. I became consumed by my pursuits, neglecting other essential aspects of self-care. The act of juggling became an addiction, an endless cycle of over-working, burnout, and recovery in the form of a new project.

Similar to my father, I grew increasingly desensitized to the dysfunction I was encountering, reaching a point where news that would typically be debilitating failed to evoke much of a response from me.

Why is my one self not enough for him? Who will be the next pursuit of his wandering eye? What can I do to be enough for him?

When I found myself slipping into these thoughts, I'd immediately throw up mental barricades and find something to do. If I was busy, I didn't have to feel. What I was doing felt completely healthy. Why would immersing myself in something that hurts give me any benefit? However, it's in the hurt places we start the healing process.

At this point in my life though, I adapted by redirecting my attention away from emotional situations instead of directly confronting them. I was unaware of the hardening of my emotional barriers and how much this could affect not only my future relationships but my work, life, and views.

As time passed and new opportunities arose, the need for change settled in and I found the strength to turn the page and leave that chapter of my life. One difficult break-up later, and the outreached hand of a childhood friend, I found myself in a completely different circus. I moved about an hour away from my hometown Dixon, to Lincoln, California, and it was here that I was not only encouraged to slow down, but was forced to stop any kind of work altogether, with the emergence of the COVID-19 pandemic.

It was a difficult adjustment to make but it was smoothed over by the gentle presence of my new housemates, overfamiliar with my overworking-to-burnout habits, having known them since elementary school. I felt unsettled and a little lost as many did in this international time of confusion. I was in a new city with new people, and soon began a new job while my family was now states away, having moved to Texas.

I found temporary purpose in my new job as a legal assistant at a nearby law firm. Along these ups and downs, I wasn't exactly aware of my use of work to mask my vulnerability. With each bump in the road, working was what I subconsciously clung to.

Within this new job, it became clear this would not be a lasting position as I recognized the shallow work of this particular business did little to fulfill my creative and restless needs. I observed the turnover within the law firm, witnessing colleagues come and go like transient performers in an ever-changing circus. My workload doubled with each peer that left but yet I stayed, filling my days, evenings, and some weekends with the dreary paperwork and cold calls. I tried to keep it interesting by working outside of my scope to innovate ways of streamlining work and boosting efficiency. This may have been my way of compensating the lack of fulfillment my job gave me, by doing more. Choosing quantity over quality. It also says alot about my willingness to stretch myself thin to keep something working that is not entirely functional.

I soon worked my way to a promotion switching into a different department. This minor boost of status, with almost no pay increase, still ignited my passions of problem-solving with the little recognition I was given. Similar to my odd jobs as a kid, it was just enough to make me feel appreciated and keep me willing to work. I was serving a cause I did not necessarily resonate with, but I received a smidge of purpose, from the weight I had taken on for the sake of this company. I made myself feel that I fit in there, even though I was really freefalling in my personal life.

My promotion, a moment of triumph, was soon tinged with the realization that it stemmed from necessity rather than genuine recognition. In other words, it wasn't about me or my performance at all. The firm was overworking and underpaying just about every member of its staff and my innovative tactics were becoming expected instead of rewarded. Superiors demanded seemingly life-devotion to these minimum-wage positions and most of us were not having it. The jester's act, once applauded, now felt like a precarious balancing act on a tightrope, threatening to plunge myself and those around me into burnout.

I felt slightly used and, at this point in time, began to question who I was and what kind of purpose I was even searching for.

An Illusion of Balance

It wasn't long before I began to grasp at new colorful juggling pins, seeking solace and purpose amidst chaos. Yoga teacher training, online courses in business and legal studies, and even pursuing a Private Pilot's License became part of the spectacle, all beside my job in the law firm that never slept. The new additions to my act were a great creative break from the monotonous work as a legal assistant and still provided the distraction I desperately needed in order to not face the vulnerability of feeling suspended in the unknown of this new life chapter.

I found that some of these newfound skills, such as a deeper understanding and practice of yoga as well as education in business, were leading my journey into yet another direction that I was happily following. It was at this time that I found an anchor and comfort zone in the form of my now life partner, Cameron.

When I was introduced to Cameron it was through a mutual friend, Julia Noble. Julia and I have shared a deep friendship for many years. She possesses an uncanny intuition that's often been spot on. When she told me one day that she had a great guy she wanted me to meet, I trusted her instinct. It's clear now that had she introduced him at any other moment, things might not have aligned as they did.

Cameron was a great guy indeed. He was someone who could see through this illusion of balance I portrayed to the public and had a deep understanding of my restlessness as a form of diversion.

The world was still in the midst of the pandemic, so Cameron and I were not able to see much of each other in person. However, we found ourselves becoming quickly acquainted and talking on the phone for the majority of everyday. As we got to know each other, we came to find out we had actually met one another long before Julia introduced us. Our mothers had been friends when we were kids, and even found an old picture of us when we were little.

Something about this connection we shared gave me a deep sense of trust in our path together. It allowed me to see that everything happens for a reason. Although we had apparently known each other before, and even gone to the same high-school briefly, I was not yet ready to meet my person yet and he was not either. Whatever you believe in, the timing of the universe, fate, God, I knew that our time was now and it was right.

This isn't to say we immediately lived happily ever after and walked off into the sunset. Very far from that, actually. It was tasking to begin a new relationship with the barriers I had unknowingly put up. I felt as though he was asking too much of me when it came to anything more than surface-level communication or commitment. I had compromised so much of myself with past partners that I found myself fighting any compromise posed to me. I had adopted selfish traits in an attempt to protect my peace and not fall into another rocky relationship. There was much we had to learn about each other and habits I needed to break for myself. Although I believe he was set into my path for a reason, I had to learn to love and understand myself, to love him in the way he deserved.

Cameron offered me a bubble of safety and support that led me to make the jump from my demanding and undervalued position in the legal field to opening my own business that we built together.

More spinning pins than ever before were being propelled into the air as Cameron and I moved back to our hometown of Dixon, California, and I stepped up to the challenge of creating Busy Bee Yoga, my brick and mortar yoga studio. Creating and running a yoga studio was a sharp contrast to my structured corporate job. Unbeknownst to me, this total shift in direction was something I had been inadvertently desiring. Yoga symbolized health, balance, and intention, all the things I had been lacking but obviously was drawn to. The business fueled my restless passion, taking me on an alternative journey and provoking my creative senses to bring something new and good to my city.

I started to tackle this project the way I knew best, putting my waking hours to work and going into overdrive. I was ironically starting a business of health and intention from a somewhat unhealthy and confused place.

The Making of Busy Bee Studios

In a city known for its strong sense of community and rooted traditions, establishing a new business was intimidating especially with the services I planned to offer. I started small in a space that doubled as a personal office for a loan officer, Karstin Stranger. Karstin swiftly became my business mentor, who's guiding hand would lead me to the success I have experienced with the studio, today.

This original space could fit about four yoga mats, but even that was generous. Operations started quietly, by mere word-of-mouth, once I set the date for our first yoga class. I tirelessly planned each component of the act I was to set to perform and orchestrate for my students. From breathing cues to the stretches, the music I would play, how bright the lights should be, how I should greet them and how I would conclude, I obsessed over the details, wary of scaring a potential customer away. I wanted to make the class enriching to those attending, to challenge their perspective and get them to fall in love with the practice of yoga. I integrated a series of backbends and twists that I was sure would be a big hit.

When the day came to teach my first class, one of the students was expecting, and late within the second trimester of pregnancy. Twists and backbends are usually a prenatal yoga no no, so frantically within my mind I scrapped that class plan and came up with something else entirely while holding my professionally serene mask intact for my audience.

I was only slightly becoming aware that I was falling into a similar pattern. This new start I was making for myself was actually becoming yet another environment of stress and obsession. I was taking the route of brute force and workaholism to an industry that it had no place being in. Rather than cultivating my business with intention and well-being in mind, I found myself mechanically navigating through projects without genuine purpose.

It was only when I was teaching or taking a yoga class I began to feel some of that balance and peace. I had felt this at another point as well, when I was going through my 200-hour yoga teacher training years prior. During my training, I was surrounded by welcoming and curious individuals that made me want to be the same way. The few months we learned, trained, and taught together, were among the most comforting times I'd experienced in a while. This feeling was what I wanted to encapsulate with Busy Bee but was having difficulty finding the way to do it.

Surviving past the first 1-hour, donation-based class, intimidation with a sprinkle of imposter syndrome crept in as I realized the undertaking of what was ahead. Our little spot nestled between the longstanding businesses that had deep-rooted connections to the citizens of Dixon. The florist shop overflowing with boutonnieres and corsages for every school dance, the Dixon Tribune office getting ready to distribute that week's paper, and the beloved pubs adorning the corners with patrons spilling out the doors on weekend evenings. Throughout the city, history and tradition ran strong and, to date, no other legitimate yoga studios were ever established within those limits.

Having grown up in this town, and witnessing my parents skillfully open and operate a business of their own, I possessed an intimate understanding of this community's inner workings. I was acquainted with the proprietors of the shops, offices, and pubs, but I had elevated them to a pedestal I believed was beyond the reach of your ordinary showman.

Sweeping these feelings of doubt under a yoga mat, I chugged full-speed ahead and soon discovered that my apprehensions were unwarranted. The city hall and county clerks warmly embraced me during my visits for licenses, permits, renewals, and inquiries. Even the city paper became a steadfast ally, consistently highlighting our endeavors and accomplishments as we worked to prepare for a momentous Grand Opening.

My performance as Dixon's yoga teacher brought in a new audience, now of the entire city. Pressure rose as interest grew and before long we were looking into a bigger location to house the official business of then Busy Bee Yoga.

My sights were set on a historical building right across the street from our original location and in no time we were signing a lease and breaking ground. It was such a monumental milestone but I found myself incapable of feeling the level of excitement to match such an occasion, as the long road of cleaning and construction lie dauntingly ahead.

I realize now, just how much I told myself I'd 'celebrate later' and never really appreciated the pivotal moments I was passing. It was always about preparing for the next task at hand and never giving myself the grace and time of savoring how far I had come already.

From all my inherited and adopted traits, it became clearer that being able to assess and manage my emotions was not something I possessed. Even if it was just the emotional capacity of feeling gratitude for the journey. But who needs those kinds of traits when you're a busy business owner? Why dwell on emotional aspects when there are so many logistical decisions to be made! This mindset kept me from enjoying the journey and unfortunately kept me in a tunnel vision to my end goal.

Although overwhelmed by the pressure of my now expanded audience and the high expectations from myself and those around me, I strived to keep an upbeat social media persona as I paused the donation-based services, to build and renovate the new space with Cameron, Karstin and our amazing friends. The work was constant and endless as we completely redid the building which we were set to open for the public soon with a big Grand Opening party.

Responding to comments while sanding the floors, posting the 'Yoga Pose of the Day' while facilitating partnerships with lululemon and pressed juice, creating our website and installing mirrors. Hashtagging, painting, posting, nailing, snapping smiling selfies while mentally and physically struggling under the weight of my juggling act. I fervently worked to prove my dedication, juggling tasks and responsibilities with unparalleled enthusiasm. The act became synonymous with my identity, blurring the line between performer and person.

The day of our Grand Opening grew closer and the magic of social media was able to mask it all while creating the buzz for our upcoming party. Going into overdrive for those last finishing touches of music, decor, refreshments, and entertainment for the big day, it finally came time to open the doors.

Drowning in the Act

You would think that the insistent workload to prepare for such an occasion would trigger a sense of pride and a moment to allow myself a pause to reflect. But how could this be, when this was just the beginning?

While I did rejoice in the opening and all the wonderful things we were now able to serve our community within this space of our own, this new circus tent was now ornamented with a glaring Open sign. This signified the need for consistent management, daily instruction of classes, shopkeeping duties, and constant innovation for new business. With a staff of one, I wore the hat of all of these roles and spent my waking moments teaching, advertising, selling, cleaning, and anything else that arose as I learned the ropes of being a business owner.

I thrive when faced with lengthy to-do lists and know that if there is one thing I can do, it's putting my head down and continuing to work. However, it started to feel like it was impossible to adjust to this new stage. The juggling pins began to falter, slipping from my grasp as I struggled to find a rhythm in my work. Completing tasks was one thing, but my daily list seemed to multiply with each item I crossed off. The customer service aspect alone in running a business meant creating a specialized solution to each new problem that surfaced. I was drowning in sticky notes and reminders but didn't dwell as there was work to be done.

At this point, I don't think I was feeling anything. I had acclimatized to the stress and made it into normalcy. I was constantly moving, keeping the body busy and so, therefore, the mind. There was little intention behind my work and deep down, the need to slow down and bring intention instead of excess, was gnawing at me but I didn't listen. I wasn't necessarily distracting myself but, after years of using work as a method of distraction, I pushed myself to limits to feel in myself that I was doing enough.

Amidst the whirlwind of my act, my family saw through that painted smile of the Joker. They sensed the vulnerability masked by my busyness. Living a tranquil life in Texas, they urged me to come visit them even if it was just an excuse to plop on their couch and do nothing for a while. Their concerned voices acted as gentle reminders, cautioning me about the consequences of pushing myself too far and urging me to step back and reclaim my own authenticity.

But I persisted. Responsibilities teetered on the edge of my juggling pins, and burnout loomed like suspended objects waiting to be caught. The fear of vulnerability and the belief that I must always appear strong drove me to juggle even more fervently. Work became my escape, my shield against the turmoil of personal challenges. The juggling act provided a distraction, a way to avoid facing the emotions that threatened to unravel me.

Late on the evening of July 13th, 2022, I received a call while I was at a dinner party with some friends. It was a casual gathering, filled with laughter and joy. However, the atmosphere shifted when I answered the phone and heard the frantic voice on the other end. The colorful juggling balls flying overhead plummeted to the stage floor. A young friend of mine had tragically passed away.

Just a few weeks prior, he was bounding through the doors of my yoga studio to say hi while he was visiting from out of town. I remember his staggeringly tall presence filling our doorway as he popped his head in exclaiming, "Wow, so this is your studio!" Surprised by his visit, I ran to give him a hug and eagerly gave him a brief introduction of the space. He brushed his hands along the exercise apparel hung at the front of our shop and puttered his way back to the space where we instructed classes. "So much room for activities," he said looking around. We chatted about what he was doing in town and how long he would be here for. Talked about school, work, and weekend plans and left it off with an "I'm sure I'll see you around again before I head back home".

He was just 22 years old, full of life, one of the most extroverted, and happy-go-lucky people I knew. These characteristics so many knew him to possess now only lived in memory and this idea rocked me to my core. How could someone so young and so lively just blip from existence so suddenly?

As someone who had always struggled with showing vulnerability and managing my emotions, the news of his passing hit me like a tidal wave. I felt a sense of shock coursing through me and that pin-prick of adrenaline with every move I made as I reached out to others who were close to him. It was late at night, but I had to know what happened and if this was just a horrible rumor. Obviously, someone had to be mistaken.

No matter what happened, surely he was still alive. The most I allowed myself to believe was that he was badly injured and someone had mistaken this for him being dead.

Needing to move or do something, I got into my car and began driving towards a gathering of friends who had also heard the news. But as I drove, the weight of the emotions came crashing down upon me. It became too much to bear. I had to pull over on the side of the road, overwhelmed by intense crying, uncontrollable shaking, and a surge of shock. The sheer magnitude of the loss engulfed me, and I felt vomit begin to rise as the racing of my heart and the spinning of my mind brought nausea to the surface.

Overwhelmed with finding ways to spin this so it wasn't true, I didn't realize as his death began to trend on Twitter. The news was in fact true. Having met with a group of his friends and family at a local bar, we locked the doors and everyone fell silent as a news broadcast came across the screen drilling the permanence and tragedy of this passing into us all.

Looking around, some were trying to talk it through, some were trying to distract themselves, others were sharing funny past stories, and some sat in silence as they processed. I personally didn't know what to do with myself. I sat stirring my drink at the edge of the bar, trying to think back to other instances of people passing away and wondering why I was feeling things new and differently than before. Why did I feel so useless and heavy and lost?

It was the cruel irony of his age and his vibrant spirit being extinguished, that I couldn't fathom. This concept weighed down heavier than before when I attended the viewing of his body. I saw him lying there, motionless and serene. It was a stark contrast to the lively person I had known. The reality of his absence hit me with a force I couldn't ignore.

His passing plunged me into a deep depression. I found myself spiraling into profound thoughts about life, the purpose behind our actions, and the fleeting nature of our existence. I was reminded by many that this is exactly why life is so special because it is not permanent. But all I heard was that life is not permanent, so why do anything at all.

I slept in late most mornings keeping the curtains drawn. TV blaring, so I didn't have to sit with my own thoughts. My infinite to-do list still ever-present, but now pushed aside as I found the comfort of my bed and that episode of Sex and the City more important. It took me a considerable amount of time in therapy, once I eventually decided to go, to begin pulling myself out of the darkness. The weight of running my business, combined with the weight of my new understanding of my vulnerable capacity, became an unbearable burden.

This tragedy rattled me so deeply and forced me into emotions I didn't understand. I felt the intensity of everything I had worked so hard to put up barricades against. I had guarded myself against my own sensitivity for years and now had this crash of emotions that I didn't know how to manage. I had never taken the time to get to know myself and now I was being forced to face who that person was.

I struggled with how to feel and what to do about it for a month or two, so I did nothing. I found this unmanageable emotional side of me filling me with rage at one moment and crippling sadness the next. I was mad that in his accidental death there was no one to blame. So, instead, I turned my anger towards the people happily walking their dogs each morning, ignorant of the darkness of our world. I was mad at others for not feeling the grief and being able to keep leading their normal lives. I was sad that Cameron had to leave me to go to work each day, and sad that I could no longer feel a will to do anything but sit and contemplate the cruelty of life.

For a while there, I could not find the motivation and energy to fulfill even the minimum requirements of my job. Teaching yoga had always been a passion of mine, but now it felt like a monumental task just to show up. I tried to piece together a make-shift Joker's mask with each social setting I was forced to be in. Acting normal for just enough time, until I could return to my dark room. That was all I was capable of doing besides the occasional social media post to make everything look all fine and dandy to the public. Other business duties took a backseat until I could pull myself out of my funk that I really didn't see happening anytime soon. I hid my deep depression behind those curated social media posts, but it was evident to those who knew me well that I needed help. I needed to focus on myself and learn how to manage my emotions effectively.

Therapy was a bit weird for me starting out. It seemed pointless and exasperating just to think about explaining my whole life to someone, just to make an assessment and provide advice. I didn't want a Band-Aid, I wanted someone to hypnotize me back to a fully-functional member of society again. That was not a part of the package apparently.

I kept myself accountable, showing up to the weekly meetings and from each one came little homework assignments and tactics to implement when I began to feel anxious or depressed. We talked through the certain limiting beliefs that I held within and how to reframe that mindset. You would think it would be apparent to me at this point, but together we learned and brought to light that I had convinced myself that having emotions made you weak. Because of this, I never learned to manage intense emotions such as those triggered by my friend's death.

We discussed my incessant need to work and overwork and exposed the truths behind this. I was growing each day, realizing how much I'd been compensating for the lack of self-awareness in my own life by trying to go outwards and serve others in their lives. I was learning the importance of doing inner work within yourself and that you can't properly serve others if you are not showing up as your authentic self.

I had been treating my feelings like the Joker cards in a deck, plucking them out and throwing them to the side so I could get on with the game. I taught myself over time that vulnerability was a weakness, and giving it a spotlight would take more work than necessary when there was real work to be done. With those intense emotions spilling over every which way, and my new profound concepts of life and death, I allowed myself to ponder. I had been paralyzed from it all. I struggled to make sense of any of it, leaving me stuck and drowning in the many roles and work I had taken on.

Beyond the Masquerade

It took time, but I began to recognize the masquerade. The juggling act that once defined me had become a burden, obscuring my true self. I began to prioritize my well-being and learned to create a manageable workload that allowed me time to breathe. It is a constant learning process, and there are moments when I slip back into old habits of overworking. However, through my experiences, I recognized the importance of personal time and self-care.

I understood that I couldn't serve my community to the best of my ability if I wasn't showing up as my genuine self. Taking care of my own mental and emotional health became a priority, and I strived to manage my emotions regularly instead of pushing them aside until they brought me to a breaking point.

Starting that journey towards healing and fixing my learned and adapted traits, I found I do not need to take the burden of every possible problem I come across immediately. I no longer need to take up new projects and blind myself with work for the sole purpose of distraction or other people's approval. Growing my team, I now have the support of additional instructors, shop managers, as well as a decent therapist, loving friends and family in my corner.

Through my journey, I have learned the power of sensitivity, the importance of seeking help, and the significance of living an authentic life. I have come to understand that the purpose behind the things we do, lies in our ability to connect with ourselves and others on a deeper level. Life is fragile and fleeting, and it is essential to embrace each moment and appreciate the relationships we have. The pain of losing my friend will always remain, his passing served as a wake-up call, urging me to reassess my priorities and learn to care for myself. It was a profound lesson that allowed me to grow and find strength within my vulnerability.

Now, standing on a different stage, I reflect on the lessons learned from my jester's performance. I continue to work on myself, recognizing that self-discovery and self-care are ongoing processes. I have cultivated a support system that encourages me to take time for myself and provides a safety net when I need it. The burden of every single responsibility no longer weighs solely on my shoulders.

By the time this book reaches you, Busy Bee Yoga will have expanded into its third location and rebranded to Busy Bee Studios, a fitness and community center. Busy Bee Studios allows a space for all the busy individuals in the area to have a healthy and creative outlet to the stresses and anxieties of life.

Through yoga, exercise, fundraisers, quirky workshops, and mixers, we strive to create opportunities for every bee. From our kids yoga and moms fitness classes, to our senior classes and community outreach programs, our studio opens the door to anyone's ideas and needs.

Along the way, I have also co-founded a second business venture; Maganda Media Management, a full-service social media agency that aids in the creation and management of personal brands to showcase the beauty of your authentic self.

The props and tricks of the jester no longer define me individually. I embrace the beauty of simplicity, letting go of the need to juggle it all. As I step into my role as a yoga instructor, or media manager, or author, I do so with a renewed sense of purpose. I understand that my role extends beyond teaching postures or posting pictures. It involves holding space for myself and individuals to genuinely connect and grow.

I am grateful for the journey that led me to this point, even though it was born out of many difficult hurdles of varying sizes. Through my own healing and growth, which will be a continuous journey, I hope to inspire others to prioritize their well-being and embark on their own paths of self-discovery so they can apply this into better serving others.

The jester's mask now lies discarded and although life will always present its share of challenges and losses, by embracing vulnerability, seeking support, and staying true to ourselves, we can navigate the complexities with grace and resilience. And in doing so, we honor those we have lost and carry their memories within us as a reminder to live fully and authentically.

KATRINA MARSH

Katrina Marsh is an ambitious female entrepreneur that lives by the guidelines of her personal philosophy; Embrace Authenticity, Foster Community, and Cultivate Curiosity. Raised in Dixon, a small town in Northern California, Katrina's early years were marked by a quest for purpose. In 2020, she earned her first Associates Degree in Business Administration and another in Legal Studies, along with a Certificate in Paralegal Studies in 2021.

Her passion for learning drove her to obtain a 200-Hour Yoga Teacher Certification, leading her to explore holistic health and ultimately found the first yoga studio in her city. Since its creation in 2021, the yoga studio has evolved into Busy Bee Studios—a versatile wellness and community hub. In 2022, Katrina co-founded Maganda Media Management, a full-service media agency focused on curating authentic personal brands for individuals and businesses alike. Through these endeavors, Katrina intertwines her commitment to self-discovery and growth by building a community of dedicated and curious individuals. Katrina is devoted to inspiring young minds to embark on their own journeys of self-discovery, encouraging them to unearth their passions and utilize their gifts in service to others.

www.hellotherekatrina.com

9

CHANGE YOUR DESTINY

BY BETH A. BOLES

I've heard it said that life is what you make of it. But what happens when life is like a roller coaster ride that you can't get off? It keeps going around and around the same pattern of thrills and pain. My life, it seems, has been about making life happy for everyone else at the expense of my own health, finances and well being. I have always had a deep longing in my soul to create a beautiful life for those closest to me. In an effort to help others, I made some poor decisions. I became a facilitator and an enabler, thinking if I gave enough material possessions that it would somehow make them happy and love me.

I tried to fill the void in myself by trying to fill the void or unhappiness of those around me. Unable to set clear boundaries for myself and the relationships in my life, I took on the emotional, physical and financial responsibilities of others close to me as my own. My empathy has been a blessing and a curse, because I am just now learning to be more responsible with this gift after a lifetime of pain and heartache.

I am Beth A Boles, owner of B'Dazzled Boutique, a successful thriving ladies' boutique in Pendleton, Indiana. I have always had great empathy for others in business, family and friendships. My intense desire to 'fix' everyone's life has been costly and exhausting, mentally and physically. After two failed marriages, the death of my oldest son, and constant high stress, I have finally realized that other people's happiness is not always my responsibility, but the lesson almost cost me everything.

This is my story.

Running On Empty

My parents divorced when I was a child. Their long-distance relationship and divorce was traumatic for me. There was constant emotional turbulence and I often felt abandoned and unloved by them. This deep hurt caused me to look for love in all the wrong places. I moved out of home when I was 17, to work and make my own life, because I wanted to be independent and make my own choices, for better or worse. Because of my abandonment issues, I was rebellious and many times out of control. Soon after high school, I met my first husband and was pregnant and married very young. In my mind, I thought a man and a child could fill my feeling of emptiness and my aching need to feel loved. I enjoyed being a Mom and working, so a couple years later I welcomed my second son into the world. Life was difficult financially and I began feeling that there was more in store for me in life than the jobs I was doing at that time. Is this all I'd ever be?

I called my Mom and stepdad and asked if I could move my family to Oklahoma and try to start a new and better life. So, after some debate between my husband and myself, and an ultimatum, my husband, my two year old, my newborn boy and I packed up everything and every cat, dog, chicken and duck we owned, to travel across the country to work for my parents and learn a new trade as a picture framer and ranch hand. Finances were tight, so I had to work full time, take care of babies, dishes, laundry, mowing and help with the horses. My husband worked as well and it was not easy to make ends meet. No matter what I did, it seemed I could not make my husband happy. He and I both worked long hours, but neither of us seemed to be satisfied or able to make ends meet. He felt resentful over the move to Oklahoma and giving up his life and family in Indiana. The arguments got louder and more frequent and the distance was growing. Young love is difficult, because neither person has experience and many hurtful words can be said in anger and in the heat of the moment. After several years, my husband and I decided to move back to Indiana, closer to his family and friends, try to start over and save the marriage.

I started as a waitress, but soon realized I was a horrible one! I switched to retail, selling ladies' clothing as a co-manager, then a manager. I learned many valuable business strategies and lessons there, but I still felt I was capable of so much more than this. Then, a light went on in my mind and, with the help of my stepdad, opened my own picture framing business in my husband's small town. I loved my job and my customers, but it was extremely hard work and I carried a lot of the stress and expenses on my shoulders. I worked six-day weeks, did expos and missed many precious moments with my two boys, thinking it was the right thing to do. I somewhat felt like a martyr. I'd sacrifice myself for the good of the family. I did not realize then that a healthy family works together to make the work lighter and the stress more bearable.

Life is so difficult to manage when both parties feel like they are unappreciated and alone in the marriage. Even though my husband worked a job and helped make picture frames in the evenings, I felt overworked, unappreciated and unloved. I just want a 'thank you' and a hug. I longed for him to see my sacrifices and hard work. I wanted him to see I was suffering and care enough to just hold me, but there was too much resentment in both of us. After 16 years, the marriage ended and my world changed. I was exhausted and had nothing left to give him or anyone else at this time. I just felt numb and shattered. This caused a deep anxiety within myself. I never thought I'd be divorced, because I thought he was my best friend. I woke up one day and realized best friends work equally at work, home and in relationships. I do not place blame as he and I were married so young, and it was a mutual failure to understand one another's needs, but staying in an angry home was not an option any longer. I'd start over and be free of the mental and emotional stress, but freedom only comes with power over emotions.

Looking back, I realize I was a bad listener and took things into my own hands. If I did not get my way, I'd throw a tantrum until he capitulated to my will. I made some bad choices at home and in business, which caused a chasm between him and me. I worked hard at work and at home, but I blamed him internally for not taking care of me. He resented me for being so headstrong and independent. This caused him to be angry and cold to my needs. In truth, I just wanted a hug and for him to see me as a woman and not his caregiver or enemy. I told myself I would never let this happen in the future.

The Cycle Continues

I moved in with a girlfriend, who quickly became my bestie, with all four of our kids. The single life began and it was an adventure every day. She and I had so much fun and did so many things on the bucket list together. It was also wonderful to share the parenting load with another woman and feel appreciated. The kids enjoyed the extended family unit and all seemed well in the world. It was during this time that I realized that I still had a hole in my heart and felt like I needed a man to fill that void. It was in those dark nights, when my heart was racing and sleep would not come, that I craved the closeness of a romantic relationship. Then like it was fate, there was my second husband. However, not everything that feels right is the truth. Discernment is key.

But at this time, I hadn't learned to not just follow the heart, but to analyze with the mind and to know that actions speak louder than words. He was visiting from Germany and seemed so kind and affectionate, which I longed for inside my heart. He seemed to be everything my little heart yearned for and he also seemed to accept and enjoy my teen boys. Only everything is not as it appears on the surface. I ignored so many red flags. After a year of expensive flights and phone calls, it was agreed that I would close my well known picture-framing business and move to Germany with my boys, a promise of marriage, job and a beautiful new future. So I thought. It was an illusion that my heart created and my mind refused to see the warnings and ignore the facts.

Surprise! The week of my arrival, I was not feeling well, so I took a quickie home pregnancy test. It was positive. The news of my third son did not go down well with my future husband. He turned his back on me that day, leaving me disillusioned and heartbroken to my core. He waited weeks to get me a doctor appointment and refused to tell his parents. He even made me fake an illness and hide under blankets on the couch to hide my belly. I was mortified and in shock. This man was not the man that I made up in my own mind, and the future I also pretended it would be. Everytime I mentioned marriage, he would get furious and refuse to talk about it. Where did my kind loving man go? Despite the strained relationship, I brought my teen boys over to Germany, after I started working for him in his firm and making an income again. I was determined to get married and create a happy family, despite all odds. It felt surreal. It felt like I was an actress playing a part in a horrible film. I went from owning my own business and running my own life, to living in a foreign country with little money and a language barrier. I had no car and my sons and I walked everywhere, unless my unpredictable boyfriend happened to be home with the car. My oldest son stayed and excelled in German school, despite a turbulent relationship with my future husband. My youngest teen did not want to live in Germany under these conditions and left to live with his dad in America. It hurt so bad in my heart. I would wake up with panic attacks. I cried every single day.

Despite hardships, I am normally a very happy-hearted person, so this was not my personality. I try to see everything and everyone in a positive way and feel like God made me for this very reason. I feel joy lifting the spirits of others, while many times ignoring my own pain. Perhaps this is my way to cope with my own issues. However, trying to heal or fix others, I now realize, does not repair my own wounds or take the place of true peace within myself.

Even with all the tension and animosity, my second husband and I married soon after the birth of my third son. I thought this would make him open his eyes, love me, see my worth and accept his baby boy. I was miserable in Germany. I was so isolated, hopeless and struggling with my own self-esteem, that my oldest teen son could barely recognize his mother anymore. He kept asking, "Where is my Mom?" I had no answer, I was lost. I would walk into the woods with my little dog, sit down and cry at my demise. How did I let myself get here? He only knew me as an independent, outgoing and strong-willed woman. There was constant hostility and arguing at home. Many times, my new husband would leave me with no explanation. I would panic and sometimes walk the brick streets of Germany looking for a sign of him or his vehicle. This was very upsetting for my son to watch and he felt powerless to save me. He got very upset one night when my husband and I were once more in a heated argument, and had it out with my husband. The German police were called and there was a three-day separation. My oldest son just wanted his Mom treated like a princess, not like a worthless possession, constantly being put down or hurt from insults. My son saw me work a job, take care of the baby, do the housework and cook, with no appreciation or acknowledgement. He stayed over three years and then moved back to America, to get away from the constant stress, leaving me without his emotional support. Then next shock, I was pregnant with a miracle baby boy number four - at 39 years old! I was literally losing my mind with loneliness and feeling unloved, so in desperation to save my marriage and myself, I opened a small boutique in Germany where I finally learned the German language and made friends. I made some lasting relationships there and am thankful to this day for the people the Lord sent my way.

My life was still a loveless torment of long work days full of sadness and a deep pit of despair in my gut. I would spend much time confiding my deepest thoughts to my Mom and a few good friends by email. It seemed, once more, that I was incapable of making my husband happy or content. I tried everything my mind could think of to have this man see me, the real me, and relate to me as a person. I worked full time and also helped my husband in his business. I would spend hours sending emails and attending expos to help him make his business grow into the thriving establishment it is today. I did all the housework, worked in the yard, got most of the groceries, cooked and raised the baby alone most of the time. It was hard for me to imagine caring and raising two children with the minimal help I got from my husband. He and I went to a counselor and an agreement was made between us that he would help me more when our next son was here. My fourth son was born, the truth apparent that I was once again in this with little help, so I started to make my exit plan. After close to 4 years of my personal hell on earth, I told my husband and his parents that the two babies and myself would be moving back to America without my husband. His father agreed with this decision and, to this day, I do not know what his mother thought, but no one tried to stop me.

This was not taken lightly, but in my heart and mind this time, I knew what I had to do. I would start all over again. The day I got on the plane, I could feel the hand of God on my shoulder and I knew He would walk beside me during this difficult time. I knew what it was like to start from nothing and build a life, so I was confident in my abilities to overcome huge obstacles and survive. I had no choice but to succeed. When you have run out of every option, it is 'do or die' time. There is no margin for failure when you have two babies that depend on you.

For years, the thought of leaving my husband would make my gut curl and cause me to lose my breath. It was like so many times that he left me in anger, tears would flow and sheer panic would set in my entire body. Why was I so afraid he would leave me and never come back? I had to get a grip on my emotions and be strong for my children and the future for all of us. I would overcome my insecurities and walk boldly into an adventure that would allow me to be independent financially, and free from the mental torture of not being truly loved or seen.

I felt invigorated and full of purpose when I finally made my move.

On a Wing and a Prayer

With the help of dear friends, hard work and determination, I opened a small picture frame shop/boutique in Pendleton. I was told by many that it would never succeed in this small town, but I knew God was in me. It was like a miracle when my kind new landlord kept the store rent low and also rented me a little upstairs apartment across the street that I could afford. I was very low on funds and had to be very creative to find ways to make money. I painted both the boutique and apartment by hand and it felt good to make something beautiful. I would walk with the babies, pick up sticks and either Duck tape or paint them for decorations. I shopped for clothes at the local consignment shop for myself and had a very small wardrobe. I had to invest every penny I could back into my business. I did expos, church shows and festivals, then I started first on Facebook posting pictures of the boutique, which changed the dynamics of my business quite quickly. I got some negative feedback using Facebook for business but, for the most part, I got great comments and a lot of new customers. The good far outweighed the bad for sure. I worked constantly at the shop and at home on my business. As much as possible, given that I had my babies to care for daily. I was so very grateful the day a good friend agreed to help me part time. I was frail from all the stress of Germany and the self-inflicted malnutrition from the pregnancies there, trying to stay slim and beautiful for my husband to love me. This caused my body to revolt and cause me pain and constant exhaustion.

It was taking its toll on my body carrying two babies, laundry and groceries up a steep flight of stairs. Sometimes, halfway up, I would just sit and cry. To top it all off, I broke my finger while lifting weights, which made everything even more difficult for months. Oh happy day when my sweet landlord found a ground-floor duplex that I could afford since the boutique was growing each week. I was thankful and celebrated every single customer and sale, many times doing a silent happy dance behind the counter. These wonderful people were literally supporting my little family and it warms my heart to this very day. The business started to get noticed and I was on my way to becoming a profitable company and asset to the community. Sometimes, if your eyes are open, you will see that God sends 'angels' and 'messengers' through people. I have witnessed and seen this time and again in my own life.

Then, after over three years of living separately but always in contact, my second husband made his big move to America to be with me and his two boys. I helped him become a permanent resident, thinking he would be a changed man here in my own country. It started okay, as he opened his own business, importing furniture and home decor to resell out of a retail space. However, it wasn't long before he became bored with his new line of work, so he sold out most of his goods and I moved into his larger retail building. It was a very unhealthy relationship and more like a business partnership. It still didn't feel right and I still felt unloved by him. I prayed for years for an answer, but it seemed like my prayers went unanswered as my husband got more depressed and unhappy in his life with me and America. He was so homesick and completely miserable here. He poured his emotions into alcohol and started working less and less hours. I was the primary earner and I poured my heart and soul into my business which was growing by leaps and bounds. B'Dazzled Boutique was the place to be for shopping fun! I loved my job, my employees and the long hours. My work kept my mind in a creative, happy space and away from facing emotional issues. I thought if I was successful enough and financially independent that I would be in a better place, not needing a man for anything. I never wanted to be hurt so badly ever again. I would build walls around myself to become everything my husband thought I could never be. I could live without him.

But once again, I thought if I worked and provided enough that I could make my husband and kids happy. I would give and give until I was acknowledged and loved as I desired in my heart. Many times, I would be left behind to work while he and the boys took off early to the lake or went off somewhere to have fun. I would even encourage this many times, thinking it would somehow change his mind about me. I still to this day do not realize why I wanted this one person's love and approval so much, that I was willing to destroy my own health and peace. Someone had to be responsible though, and that had always been me and still continues to this day. The resentment between us grew and the marriage, that was not built on a firm foundation, started to crumble.

Out of the Ashes

In the midst of a marriage in turmoil and seven-day work weeks, my whole world came crashing down on me. After experiencing side pains and being diagnosed with a hernia, my eldest son could not get out of bed and was writhing in pain. I rushed him to the ER where he was found to have a large tumor that had exploded in his intestine. Emergency surgery, cutting him vertically and permanently, was only the beginning of the nightmare. At 24, my son had aggressive cancer. My heart and mind were in disbelief at his condition. I was sure he could overcome this illness and I honestly had no idea how dire the situation was in his case. I now had to juggle shock, doctor appointments, hospital visits, chemo sessions, a business, husband and young boys at home. Pure horror and dread filled my entire being as I watched my big strong boy deteriorate before my very eyes. He would look at me with fear and anxiety and ask me what to do. I would always try to encourage him and give him hope. My mind and heart could not accept the disease and that he might leave me. He and I believed in his healing, until the very last day. I tried everything I could to be all things to all people during this time and put a smile on my face, while all the while crying out to God to help my son. I had always believed in God, but it was in these moments that my

Faith was truly tested more than anything in my life. My beautiful son was losing his battle quickly and had much suffering and pain. The Lord was my solace and my comforter, but my heart was shattered in a million pieces. I prayed over my son and with him, but I felt powerless. I looked in my son's eyes and I told him I loved him and he told me, "not as much I love you." This moment is etched into my memory, along with the many tears he and I cried together.

It is written that God is close to those who mourn and of this I am certain. People would show up at the right time when I needed a hug. A stranger felt a calling and came in to give me a word of love and support from above. Over and over, little miracles happened that would send shivers up my spine and leave tears of thankfulness streaming down my face. My precious Mom would always answer her phone and listen to me cry at my powerlessness to change my son's lethal circumstances. His last day on Earth was spent with his family and friends around him, laying on my lap, while I showed him photos of his life and reminded him of all the lives that he influenced and changed over the course of his time here. He fought death that day, but took his last breath in my arms with a single tear down his cheek. He was not ready to leave this life and start his new heavenly adventure. I will never forget the feeling of his soul leaving his Earthly body and leaving it empty. The low guttural ache cannot be explained unless experienced in person. I did not know how I would ever recover or have joy again.

My life as I knew it was over. I screamed in agony for the Lord to carry my grief. Gut-wrenching cries of sadness overcame me until He answered my prayer. I gave myself completely to Him that day, my face on the floor. I had nowhere to go, nowhere to run. The Lord was my only refuge. Each day after, He gave me small glimpses of Heaven. Whether it be a person or a sign from above, I knew it was from Him. He gave me words, when I had no words. He gave me a song, when I could not sing. He gave me Hope that even though my son is no longer here, he's waiting happily on the other side of the veil.

The tragedy of my son's death totally upended the priorities in my life, but it also gave me a purpose and a vision far above myself. It led me to a stronger faith and a more thoughtful daily walk.

The Least of These

Many times God uses broken people that have experienced tragedy to help mend other hurting people in their time of need. I went back to work quickly after my son's passing and tried my best to share my story with people I felt needed encouragement and hope. I used my pain and Faith to fuel my desire to help others going through grief or illness.I visited nursing homes and hospitals. I gave out head wraps to chemo patients, along with care packages that my friends and I put together for cancer patients. I read books about Heaven and shared my own spiritual experiences with anyone I felt needed to hear it. Anything I could do to make someone else feel hope. During this time of transformation, I still could not resolve my issues with my husband, however, and the marriage continued to grow cold. After constant arguments and unresolved trauma, the relationship ended after 16 years.

The inner peace when that trauma bond was broken, and the divorce was finished, was like a huge weight off my shoulders. I was ready to start over again with my three boys and my business. Through all the stages of my life, from the good to the bad, I can see the hand of God upon me. When I pray now, I see answers. It's not always in my time or how I expect, but He always comes through for me. It is only because of my Faith, that I can have joy through tears and laughter through fears. Without the belief that God cared for me, I do not believe I could have lived this far or had any quality of life. I take all my hurts, anger and anxiety to Him and let Him refill my heart with His strength and peace. Each day, I learn to become more at peace with myself and with others. I spend time reflecting on my past decisions and try to make better personal choices for the future. I truly desire to be the best me, for my God, myself and those around me. I react less and think more deeply about the outcome of my words.

It's been 8 years since my son took his last earthly breath and started his new life on the other side. It is this image that carries me and encourages me to always do my best and fight the good fight. Always pushing forward and never giving up, even when things look or feel impossible. I try to honor him and my other loved ones watching from above by doing the right thing, even if it is difficult. This is how I live my repurposed life. I examine myself constantly and try to correct negative thoughts or words. I believe each day, each moment is a gift. I try my best to live by the standards that I speak or write about. It is not just about saying, but actions. The old saying that actions speak louder than words is so very true.

I did not expect to have a man in my life again. I was afraid to let my walls down and get hurt once more. But thank God, He had another plan for me.

I started working out, eating healthier and taking time to rest. It was such a blessing to take more time to sit on the couch and watch movies with my boys or sing a fun song on TikTok. It felt good to smile and laugh once more. It was during this time that I started modeling for my own boutique more often and a handsome, single man sent my picture a heart. I checked out his social media page and returned a couple of post likes. He messaged me quickly and he and I have never been apart since then. I call it a Godcidence. He and I could not be more thankful or happy to have one another. A man of Faith that I can admire, love and trust with all of me. God is at the core of the relationship and it is built on solid ground.

I am blessed beyond words with my new husband and true soulmate. God sent me a love that I have never experienced before in my lifetime and I could not be happier than I am at this moment. I now know what a marriage with mutual respect and admiration feels like and it fills my heart with gratitude. He and I have a new granddaughter to cherish and love, along with my boys and his boy. Every piece just fell into place like it was formed in Heaven. I absolutely love my work at the boutique and the customers that God gives me on the daily. I am grateful I have employees to help share the work and laughter with and also, at times, some tears or fears.

With all the ups and downs over the last decade, B'Dazzled Boutique remains an outrageous success and I am humbled and blessed to be a part of it. When I think of the course of my life and all the times it seemed so dark, it makes me appreciate the genuine peace and happiness I have now. There are so many times I look back, see the chances I took or the grief I faced, and know that if it wasn't for my belief in God and my personal fortitude that I would not be here today. Living in the now, appreciating this very moment I was given, has allowed me to give and receive more blessings and love than I could have ever dreamed or asked for in my heart. Each new day is a gift and an opportunity to share Faith, Hope and Love.

BETH A. BOLES

Beth A Boles is the owner and founder of B'Dazzled Boutique in Pendleton, Indiana for over a decade. A fabulous brick and mortar store front, including a unique App, live sales and website.

Beth A Boles currently employs ten amazing employees of all ages at B'Dazzled Boutique and has a large social media and local following in central Indiana.

Beth A Boles has been a creative and evolving entrepreneur since her early twenties with a will and desire to encourage and uplift others using her life and business skills in her daily walk of faith, family and work. She strives daily to make a positive mark in her corner of the world and media outlets.

www.Bdazzledshop.com

ABOUT WOMEN THRIVE MEDIA

Women Thrive Media - Women Thrive is a global media platform where every woman has a voice. Where every woman's story is celebrated. We recognise the impact and contribution that women make in the world, and our mission is to build a platform where every woman feels included, celebrated and proud to be part of a community like this.

We started our mission work in 2017 and have since grown to an international platform of over 600k women worldwide. Over the years, we have hosted many amazing and life-changing events, had 100s of inspiring international speakers take our stage, and thousands of attendees' lives changed or impacted by our work.

Now we pride ourselves on being an inclusive platform where women looking for guidance, support and mentorship, can come and connect with others who have already walked the walk and able to share their knowledge and wisdom. Be it through our podcast, events, book, or monthly Women Thrive magazine.

Our mission is to reach 1 MILLION women every year and create a global impact on women's empowerment because we believe that if one woman is given the confidence, tools, and resources to rise, she will go on to empower thousands more. We have seen time and time again when we, as women, come together, the impact and ripple effect is so much more powerful than a woman trying to make an impact on her own.

We hope you join our community, mission, and future events.

www.womenthrivesummit.com

www.womenthrivemagazine.com

PAY IT FORWARD PAGE

If you enjoyed this book, please consider passing it to another woman that needs to hear these stories...

Tell them:

What was your favourite story?

What are your biggest take aways?

Who do you want to pass this book onto and why?

Tell them:

What was your favourite story?

What are your biggest take aways?

Who do you want to pass this book onto and why?

Tell them:

What was your favourite story?

What are your biggest take aways?

Who do you want to pass this book onto and why?

Made in United States
Orlando, FL
02 November 2023